The Arts of Peace

ALSO BY TWO RIVERS PRESS POETS

Paul Bavister, *Miletree* (1996)
Paul Bavister, *Glass* (1998)
Paul Bavister, *The Prawn Season* (2002)
Kate Behrens, *The Beholder* (2012)
Adrian Blamires, *The Effect of Coastal Processes* (2005)
Adrian Blamires, *The Pang Valley* (2010)
Joseph Butler, *Hearthstone* (2006)
Terry Cree, *Fruit* (2014)
Jane Draycott and Lesley Saunders, *Christina the Astonishing* (1998)
Jane Draycott, *Tideway* (2002)
Claire Dyer, *Eleven Rooms* (2013)
John Froy, *Eggshell: A Decorator's Notes* (2007)
David Greenslade, *Zeus Amoeba* (2009)
A. F. Harrold, *Logic and the Heart* (2004)
A. F. Harrold, *Flood* (2009)
A. F. Harrold, *The Point of Inconvenience* (2013)
Ian House, *Cutting the Quick* (2005)
Ian House, *Nothing's Lost* (2014)
Gill Learner, *The Agister's Experiment* (2011)
Kate Noakes, *The Wall Menders* (2009)
Tom Phillips, *Recreation Ground* (2012)
Victoria Pugh, *Mrs Marvellous* (2008)
Peter Robinson, *English Nettles and Other Poems* (2010)
Peter Robinson (ed.), *Reading Poetry: An Anthology* (2011)
Peter Robinson (ed.), *A Mutual Friend: Poems for Charles Dickens* (2012)
Peter Robinson, *Foreigners, Drunks and Babies: Eleven Stories* (2013)
Lesley Saunders, *Her Leafy Eye* (2009)
Lesley Saunders, *Cloud Camera* (2012)
Susan Utting, *Houses Without Walls* (2006)
Susan Utting, *Fair's Fair* (2012)
Jean Watkins, *Scrimshaw* (2013)

The Arts of Peace

An Anthology of Poetry

edited by Adrian Blamires & Peter Robinson
with an Introduction by Adam Piette

for Robert & Judith
with best wishes

Peter

5 September 2014

with the English Association

First published in the UK in 2014
by Two Rivers Press with the English Association
7 DENMARK ROAD, READING, RG1 5PA
www.tworiverspress.com

ISBN 978-1-909747-04-3

1 2 3 4 5 6 7 8 9

Two Rivers Press is represented in the UK by Inpress Ltd
and distributed by Central Books Ltd.

Cover illustration and lettering by Martin Andrews 2014
Text design by Nadja Guggi and typeset in Pollen

Printed and bound in Great Britain by Imprint Digital, Exeter.

Preface

The centenary of the beginning of what is still called the Great War, with all the ambiguities of the word 'great' in place, was bound also to focus attention on the role of poetry in that war and in relation to war. W. B. Yeats notoriously excluded war poetry from his *Oxford Book of Modern Poetry* (1936) on the grounds that passive suffering cannot make good poetry. He had previously written 'On Being Asked for a War Poem' in which he averred: 'I think it better that in times like these / A poet's mouth be silent'. His attitudes, whatever readers may feel about them today, stand as a warning against the obvious idea and the easy association. It was in such a light that the notion of this anthology began to take shape.

Among the poets we invited to contribute was Roy Fisher, who eventually told us that he couldn't write a poem because he had already written it: 'Hand-Me-Downs', which had been written during August 1993 in response to a call from Ken Smith and Judy Benson to write something for *Klaonica: Poems for Bosnia*. It has been placed first here because it too had subliminally helped shape the idea of an anthology that remembers war by concentrating its attention not on the horror, the glory, or the pity of war, but on the peace that gives war its meaning both as exception and equivocal justification.

We sent out an invitation couched in open terms, with the title of the anthology borrowed from Andrew Marvell's 'Horatian Ode upon Cromwell's Return from Ireland', where 'the inglorious arts of peace' figures as a troubling and ambiguous phrase from a similarly complex poem. As their contributions show, the indirectness of the theme for the anthology, and its mention of a century of wars, has prompted an unusually varied collection of poems, though with continuities and overlaps of topic that were neither prompted nor avoided. The anthology closes with two linked poems by Michael Longley, additions to his series of works associating classical representations of war with the present, including the recent past of what are still called The Troubles, which approached an end through a Peace Process.

For poets to mark the 1 August 1914 centenary in a collective venture is appropriate enough. The extent to which poetry has shaped our sense of the conflict is greater than for any other war, unless perhaps we include the Trojan. To make a connection between these two conflicts, ancient and modern, is not idle. Both Isaac Rosenberg and Homer make themselves felt in this volume. Heroic codes rooted in Homer's *Iliad* were exposed to the utmost scrutiny in No-man's Land and Dead Man's Dump. Yet it is not only conflict that echoes down the years, and, as Lesley Saunders' poems on Hector's helmet and Achilles' shield remind us, poetry has always also commemorated the arts of peace. Few now would join with Andrew Marvell in describing these as 'inglorious'. Few now would recommend a good war to purge a bad or debased peace. And few now would, like Rupert Brooke, seek peace *in* war.

The devastating scale of the twentieth century's two global conflicts has probably banished much of that. Poems gathered here honour the endurance and bravery of our servicemen and women, but are as troubled by notions of sacrifice and the 'glorious dead' as many of the poets, artists and reporters who bore witness to the carnage of 1914–18. Commentators may sometimes suggest that the currently living and largely non-combatant generations are somehow untested, though this is far from true for those who have experienced, as service personnel or their relatives, the more than ten years of wars in which we have been and are currently still involved. Yet all of us have seen the news reports of coffins repatriated through the village of Royal Wootton Bassett between 2007 and 2011, and we can each of us identify with the courage and skill of politicians, diplomats, and ordinary citizens in the achievement of fulfilling peace. And peace, as many of the poems sequenced together here demonstrate, *is* an art.

We are grateful to all the poets for their contributions, and for their understanding of our occasional editorial pestering. Adam Piette kindly provided an Introduction well able to draw upon the many crosscurrents and angles of approach that characterize the poems gathered here. As we know, there have even been such things as 'poetry wars', but we are pleased to report that the production of this anthology has been an entirely peaceable experience.

This publication is dependent on collaboration between Two Rivers Press and the English Association. We are grateful for the support of Pamela Bickley and Helen Lucas, to Sally Mortimore and Nadja Guggi, our managing editor and designer, and to Martin Andrews, who made the artwork that graces the anthology's cover.

ADRIAN BLAMIRES & PETER ROBINSON

Contents

Introduction

Andrew Marvell's 'An Horatian Ode upon Cromwell's Return from Ireland' sings, half-heartedly, of the need to put aside the 'inglorious arts of peace' so as to savour adventurous war. To be able to give Cromwell his due, as historical force and killing machine, lightning, falcon, hunter, the poet must put poetry aside, too, replacing it with the hollow strutting of regime propaganda. He must 'forsake his Muses dear', cease to sing 'in the shadows', and instead sing the praises of the 'active star' of the man of action. Delicately, Marvell implies the very opposite, however: and not only through the obvious irony of a poem talking about the times not needing poems.

By identifying poetry as an art of peace, we are covertly invited to read this very poem as a difficult act of peace-making as we register the ode's appalled gaze on the slaughter of the Civil War, the atrocities in Ireland, the unjustified execution of the king, the self-crowning Caesar-ism of the man of military power. Not only does Cromwell become more and more sinister as we take in the Ode's deep parliamentary sarcasms about his imperial arrogation of all power ('So much one man can do'), he begins to embody *history-as-warfare*, an indefatigably destructive force of ruin.

The Ode goes further: by ending with a complex irony about Cromwell's war-making as permanent policy ('The same arts that did gain / A power, must it maintain'), Marvell subtly sets up his own status as poet practising the arts of peace as a self-sanctioned *rival* to Cromwell and his arts of war. The Ode has power to represent, to judge through trope and tone, to counter regime propaganda with the *virtù* of its portrayal, to enter severe caveats to regime myths of war-faring power through the scope of its parodies, dissentient comparisons, its dry raillery (as when Cromwell is shown, in peacetime, still keeping his 'sword erect').

This anthology, too, in its own way maintains the power of the arts of peace into our own troubled times, questioning our sense of these days as peacetime, given the conflicts in Afghanistan and Iraq, summoning the many spectres of war memory that haunt our families, hometowns, privacies. The poems collectively enable peace to be made with the world, if only through the sense one has, once one has read through the whole anthology, that the quiet and meditative work done by these acts of crafted language offers a kind of peaceable home for the mind needing to sing in sweet shadows. Though registering the draw of the mind to war's wounds, importantly, they always also seek to deflect the gaze from the entrancements of trauma to the precious ordinariness of peace. The senior poet here, Mairi MacInnes, veteran of twentieth-century conflicts as child and as Wren, in her long recall figures to herself and to us the strange guilty innocence of pre-World War years, remembering a shoot and a screaming hare as terrible pre-figuring. With 'Ataraxia', she ponders peacefulness itself as a natural scene seemingly untroubled, yet overseen by a woman 'at the end of her tether': wars have seeped into the imagination at secret depths. Her acts of witness in this volume are at its core.

The anthology enables that deflection through various strategies of representation: some of the poems watch ex-combatant kindred peacefully gardening, as in the poems by Alison Brackenbury, Allison McVety, Isabel Galleymore, enacting 'ploughshare' transformations. Some work historically, attending to the aftermath traces of the big World Wars, Cold War, Bosnia and anti-semitic violence in current cityscapes and collective memory, as with the pieces by Steven Matthews, Derek Beaven, Tom Phillips, Terry Cree, Elaine Feinstein, Justin Quinn: variously attempting to salve cultural post-traumatic effects by cautious exorcism. That long history is given a dizzying longevity back in time in the two poems by Michael Longley here, sourcing war back to Homer, and as such the roots of European culture.

Other poems explore more intimate memories of war, Simon Smith meditating on the weave of memory and the present whilst registering the stories in the air round Manston aerodrome, Simon Frazer and Susan Utting remembering Arnhem combatants, Claire Dyer on her Great Aunt's war, Peter Robinson on his father in Second World War Italy, Jean Watkins on a Czech conscript treasuring postwar peace, Ian House imagining a sniper imagining the city he trains his sights on at peace, Kate Behrens mimicking letters home from a desert rat, Robyn Bolam and Gregory Woods registering lifelong war-bereavement in their subjects.

Other poems circle round the elegiac mode, as in the poems by Kelvin Corcoran on Ritsos, Deborah Greger on a Japanese woman at the time of Nanking, Gill Learner on Messiaen as prisoner of war, Conor Carville on the war-inflected sax playing of Karou Abe, Carol Rumens on John Rodker and Isaac Rosenberg, Angela Leighton on Rosenberg, Fleur Adcock on Anzac soldiers in the

Great War, Anthony Rudolf on a second cousin, victim of a terrible V-2 attack on Stepney, John Matthias on his wife's father and his own uncle, imagining the lice and the cold of the trenches, Jamie McKendrick on his father's war, the night sweats and revisitings, A.F. Harrold on the dead as potentially wiped from history and memory – all discovering weird political energy by such difficult acts of homage. The Troubles in Northern Ireland are figured as pacified, at last, in Gerald Dawe's vision of a fairground, William Logan's quiet appreciation of ordinariness in Belfast.

Many of the poets here strive to define peace itself: Elizabeth Smither likening it to ballet, Philip Gross sensing the ferocities enabled by fake peacetime, Adrian Blamires troping it as a precious Dead Sea scroll, Mairi MacInnes comparing it to a tide leaving 'all clear and clean and sweet', Lesley Saunders weighing the 'books of light' conjured by peaceful homes against the shield of Achilles, Vahni Capildeo measuring the double act of peace and war across history through ethnic and gender conflicts, Sean O'Brien picturing ambiguous peace as an empty room with ledger and pen, eerie space of reckoning. Other poems explore the presence of war's victims as a constant questioning of values in current culture, as with the pieces by Fred D'Aguiar and Elaine Randell.

For all the poets, poetry is itself peace-making activity: Allison McVety and John Greening comparing poems to trees from which string instruments can be made, Roy Fisher sensing the ways poems seal up ordinary life as psychic protection against conflict as sustaining story, Bill Manhire praising the 'domestic interior' of the lyric, Peter Riley enacting poetry's peaceful 'breath / against the inner ear', as of lover to lover in the calm countryside, David Morley identifying poetry with a charm to salve wounds, Michael O'Neill as equivalent to a memorial that 'renew(s) / awareness' of the power of war, Richard Price as like an intercept warning us how little our culture respects peacetime, and Peter Robinson pitching the poem as peaceful communication facing down a helicopter representing the 'forces kept in check' of the war machine, or, with 'My Italy', aligning the voices of poetry with 'just responses to our long-prolonged cries / from the states' and petty tyrants' perpetual wars'.

As an anthology published in 2014, the collection acts as a storehouse, too, of reflections on cultural memory looking back over the hundred years down to the outbreak of the Great War. Refreshingly, these poems do not labour any patriotic line on the anniversary as so much of the public remembering of the First World War has been doing. The temptation to sink to the bullying sentimentality of our own war culture is avoided too, the ridiculous circular logic that pressurizes us to justify all our little wars because 'our boys' are out there. What the whole anthology manages so well to do is to turn from anniversary-fuelled flag-waving and fake tearfulness towards a measured and felt solidarity with those who have suffered, as well as a quiet celebration of the peacetime that is so easily lost, so quickly taken for granted, so undervalued.

To preserve 'a silent belief in peace' (Peter Riley); to sustain the 'arts of peace (which) require such delicacy' (Elizabeth Smither); to foster a Quaker-inspired 'concern with the complexities of peace and peace-making' (Philip Gross): these are undertakings which cannot be confined to the private sphere, but must have their public lifelines, platforms, textual force. Poets can be reduced to leisure-time entertainers, to word-puppets performing to the tunes and drum-taps of the forces kept in check. An anthology like this reminds one that the collective voice of poets engaged in preserving peaceful attention to the world is also a political voice, speaking of solidarity with civilian pleasures and pains, countering the military-industrial complex, resisting the gravitational pull of war culture drumming away at the back of it all.

The arts of peace can stand up and speak truth to the Caesars of this world, just as they can sing of the loving energies of calm everyday time. Inglorious the arts of peace may be; but they can both judge the vainglorious warmongering warfare state, as from the shadows, and enact peacefulness through tender, tactful sharing of loving 'breath', page to eyes to mind and heart. Go, little book, go in peace.

ADAM PIETTE

The Arts of Peace

An Anthology of Poetry

Hand-Me-Downs

The nineteenth century of the bizarre
system of dates the Christians have
stands almost empty. Everybody
who helped design the first of the World
Wars is dead, no longer doing much
to anybody; likewise most of the begetters
and settlers-up of the next. They've got
clean away. And so on.

Turnips, four short rows, but enough.
Potatoes, plenty. Kale. For surplus
baby tomatoes, a jar with olive oil
an inch deep over the fruit,
then topped off with aqua vitae,
to rest on the oil and guard it. And
seal tight. And look forward
to winter. Ordinary life,
'restorable' 'normal' 'life' – paraffin,
pepper, fingers that stroke and grip –
sits in the brain like the supreme contemptuous
coinage of disease, nothing more
than a counter devised for murderers to bargain with.

ROY FISHER

Supporting Our Boys

I
Syd Ormsby put his stock up for auction,
announcing his departure for the front,
but didn't even get as far as camp
before the armistice overtook him –

bad luck or procrastination? Others
enlisted straight away: 'Anzac hero'
John Linwood did his bit and died at (where
else?) Gallipoli in 1915.

Charlie Honoré, at the farewell for
Trooper Dassler of the Mounted Rifles,
urged all the single men to volunteer
before the arrival of compulsion.

Whatever the impetus, off they marched –
names from the school roll: Smith, Clark, Dearlove, Daysh;
three from the Harris family (only
one survived); two Parkinsons; two Franklins.

In 1917 the *Waipa Post*
bemoaned the shortage of dairy farmers,
noting that fern and other second growths
were creeping into neglected pastures,

and tried to imagine the effects when
the second reserve came to be called up,
since already most of the remaining
settlers were married men with families.

Following his own call to arms, Charlie
Honoré detached himself from his wife,
his businesses, his farm, his committees,
and sailed off with the next reinforcements.

In time it would have gobbled them all up.
It even came snapping at Sam's heels, in
August 1918, with the 16th
ballot, but was just too slow to grab him.

II
Thirty or thereabouts went; all but five
came back, some in better shape than others –
young Ned Honoré spent two years dying
in Trentham military hospital.

Max Dassler was invalided home from
Egypt after serving scarcely a year,
and settled with other returned soldiers
on the Tapuohonuku block; there,

having something to prove, he was shortly
'bringing his place under in record time'.
His brother Oscar, with no such resource,
turned to the law when accused of stealing

a bag of potatoes; the magistrate,
awarding £10 damages, took note
of the ill feeling caused since war broke out
by his being 'of foreign extraction'.

Meanwhile returned Gunner Stewart, with his
war record and impeccable surname,
continued to act as cheerleader and
auctioneer at the fundraising socials.

   FLEUR ADCOCK

John Rodker: Cold Elegy for Isaac Rosenberg

no more will that pronoun in your sealed hand
nor the tricks of your verb-wires   trip me

no more shall the brush-fire   you sowed   fanned
                                 sweep by & gut my   dirt-town

   flirt on   whip of stars   red heap
         alas my lipless!
              see
your miraculum   your misillery   crackle   into closedown

CAROL RUMENS

4

Dump

'Somewhere they must have gone ...'
Isaac Rosenberg

An extramural spot walled in by wires –
   so why,
criss-crossed, cross-checked, might a gusty no-man's wind
blow liberally across that line? We're in.
   Outside,
the planed and level lands are nowhere far.
The headroom's trimmed with stripes and spiked with barbs.

Some things end here, quilted, sorted together –
   a clown's
scrapheap, collectibles fallen in lots:
white goods, wood fittings, paper, chemicals, electrics,
   set-asides
set in sidings, our saved and graded waste.
So much is ours, now full of absentness.

A trench of motley shows its patchwork of lives –
   mixed piles
of clothes, *soul-sacks*, discarded intimacies
gutted and heaped like guys, poor absentees,
   like signs
of what's not here to haunt our eyes.
Which clown's assorted losses must we stand by?

Dump – a place to guard, a word ... *Who hurled*
   them out? –
their one-time ripeness massing in a grave of scraps.
This camp of parts – where a stranger's dress, wind-lashed,
   is trapped
akimbo on the wires – exacts an epitaph:
in peace, anywhere, recall cold haunts of war.

   ANGELA LEIGHTON

Keen as are the Arrows

'If the Sky fall we shall have Larks: but who will catch them?'

A snatch of you
on Classic FM,
a smile at the thought
of your tumbling flight,
your something song
precisely caught.
I bring to it all I know
of the South Downs
killing fields,
thirty-thousand birds a day,
netted and sent to France,
how, after that War,
we lost the taste for Lark pie.
I bring to it all I know
of late spring on the Gower,
on my back, on heather,
the day marked forever
by the sudden terror
of low flyers
rehearsing for Iraq,
while something else
waited to be heard
before falling most precisely
through its own sweet song.

MAURA DOOLEY

In the Small Town ...

... of Peace, there's a splintering
cat-fight. It's Saturday night.
Magda, Kirsty, again. The lads, knee deep already
in lager and shots, wade in deeper,
and there's talk of bottlings
and big bastard uncles, and I'll have you,
pikey, cunt, you wait, and now

the morning after. Peace
has this bruised light and a headache in it.
It will have to heal
and be swept, that spilled
self-pity, the splinters that will prick and bleed
under each other's skin for weeks.

And this is peace, yes, this
is not an aberration. If the shuttered arcade
can't be rattled and still wake,
still peace, just – if only
our hushed selves will do, then it was never

Peace. Small town or seething
banlieu, in the war zone even,
peace makes its incursions. The shared fag before.
Or in the shattered stairwell,

three kid soldiers holding her,
clothes ripped, at gunpoint; one waves her away.
She's like his sister's friend, her

with the buck teeth, Magda,
was it, and the stupid laugh, but you know, he knows,

she doesn't deserve this, in the end.

PHILIP GROSS

Captain

In the ward they called him Captain,
this crazy lovely chap, presumed a man
of war at sea, not knowing the hero
come amongst them a man who flew
with Pegasus, one of a tight-knit band,
the few who *got out*. He knew not to tell,

knew simply he'd got away on a wing
and a prayer, on the toss of a coin, a wink
of the moon's lazy eye. So when they *aye-aye*-d
him, pinned on a badge and called him Captain,
he played their game – blustered, grinned,
saluted back at them, twinkled his lunatic eye.

SUSAN UTTING

Look-out

For now the city's at peace. The sniper's rifle
is upright between his knees, his hands
are soothed by the barrel and he's posted
in an armchair at a cross-roads
among dangling balconies, torn-off dresses,
jagged whisky bottles, sandbags, dolls
and listens to vanished disco tunes.
Coffee is a memory he tastes and smells.
He knows, he knows, the cafés will re-fill
with statesmen, poets, astronomers, good-time girls;
there will be public worship, evening strolls,
bookshops, bakeries, banana splits
and table scraps that can be left for dogs.

IAN HOUSE

The Colour of Soldiers

The colour of soldiers, the colour of armies in winter
The colour of flags on a hill. Shells
Of houses unroofed two centuries ago
Above the tremendous trafficking sea,
And the people expelled – what true self was lost
That wasn't again to be lost with each new place?
And the songs and legends they took, intact as yet,
And the effort that followed, to be accurate?

The sight of a kiss feels nothing like a kiss.
They say a fish knows nothing of the water.
And yet as happened, someone you barely knew
Turned up in the village trying to elicit
What kind of people we were. I saw our lives
Drawn up – clothes bought, hats and shoes,
And passports, birthdays, calendars, electoral rolls,
House numbers, timetables, surveys – no clue as to what we were!

You were always there, engaged on being –
You tell me stoutly, and I have to believe you.
I shan't wait for discovery, here you still are.
Now everyone knows, it's not at all wrong
To wander the world as a stranger. Forget
That girl at the bus-stop with her wrist tattoo
From Auschwitz or Dachau, you hadn't known her.
Though you knew her already, I'm sure.

So a sense of loss, like a door in a wall
Once plastered over, now thinly visible,
Turns into a place for the unexplained,
Floods with knowing as if a war
Needed its histories in order to be clear.
Now and then, as the tide rushes in and subsides
And leaves all clear and clean and sweet,
It follows on, our trophies from violence,
Although to understand it you must live forever.

MAIRI MACINNES

The Evacuees

Among the precious things dropped on our heads
by those clever, inventive Germans, most valued of all
was the stuff we called 'window': small strips of foil
with one side of bright aluminium, the other
matt black, unreflecting, the size of a ribbon,
thrown down in handfuls to shock the radar screens
with a storm of turbulence while the fighter planes
sneaked past the blimps, escorting the bombers –
the flying pencils, Heinkels, and Junkers –
who carried their friendly loads towards the city.
It was magical, gorgeous stuff, this 'window';
if I close my eyes I can still picture it now.
Far from the amusements of Buzzbomb Alley
and our parents' control, shipped safely away
to a countryside boarding school, we bartered scrap:
burnt-out incendiaries for pieces of shrapnel
or fragments of butterfly bomb – only vaguely aware
of what we were out of, in the purlieus of Wiltshire,
that something called 'Europe' was 'at' something called 'war'.

MATTHEW SPERLING

Twinned Villages

Tyneham, twinned with Oradour,
– in my mind at least –
its gentler, by no means less
complete annihilation
not seven months before
comes home with a cast-iron
laundry boiler, rusted thin,
where they'd take in washing
for big house and rectory ...

Above its graveyard, still in use,
the church, no charnel house
of God, but trim memorial,
comes a Sea King helicopter
hovering in navy grey,
which, like it's seeking us,
scrutinizes K-type phone-box,
wire-less telegraph pole,
reminds me, if I needed one,
of the forces kept in check
and then lifts away.

PETER ROBINSON

Where It Comes From

A sleeping commune in a far
Departement, a village the ignored
Canal ignores in passing.
The bar is never open
And the church is always shut
And no one seems to know
The names of those far hills
That stand so promisingly black
Against the slate-blue sky.
For instance. And within
This final province is a room
With pen and paper on a table
At the window, left,
It would appear, for someone else,
Who has to understand
What you can only love.

SEAN O'BRIEN

St. Michael-in-the-Hamlet

God it's ugly that church
I have a privileged outlook on
each time I trudge up north
to clock in for the ministry
of my pinched quota of care,
but ugly falls a notch short of
its dank brick and dead salmon
colour scheme, its fat jaggedly
tapering square tower topped
with oversized fake Gothic finials
in the same unappetizing
marzipannish pink that graces
the stretched ogives of its rusted
iron windows, windows missing
a few lozenges of clear glass
and ending in ventilation slats
embodged with pigeon cack.
Completed between the eruption
of Mount Tambora and
the Battle of Waterloo,
it seems to have been finished
in bloodstained lava,
and sports a skeleton of cast iron,
trademark of the builder John Cragg
who owned the Mersey Iron Foundry
and built the house I write in,
wielding weight and welding
clumpish structures skyward.
Maybe God doesn't give a damn
for churches, or good taste,
which is not to say
He doesn't have any.
He might prefer a simple heart,
a wasp's nest or a lean-to shed
to this drab steeple house
that somehow fluked a Grade
1 listing. But ugly as this church
most surely is, it's still,

worse luck, more home to me
than any mosque or duomo
in peerless travertine or marble.
Still I've other things to care about
than this, such as doling out tablets
or emptying a bottle of piss
left beside the threadbare throne
my father's realm has shrunk to,
before my name, my name is
boomed out once again
in his still undiminished bass.
The cloud of darkness
that's been gathering for months
slowly leaves his face
as he tells me of the German colonel
who'd gone scouting too close to
the English line, near Bremen,
and was blown up by a shell.
The Worcesters found him lying
on his side with multiple
fractures to all four limbs.
'Hilfe' was all he said
'fünf Tage und nichts zu Trinken.'
My father patched him up
as best he could and always
wondered if he made it,
the only German he'd felt sorry for.
In the night he shouts for my sister,
demands she call an ambulance
this minute, can't she see
the colonel's dying, he points to the floor,
it's a bloody disgrace
to leave him lying there.

JAMIE MCKENDRICK

Vermeer in Japan

after 'Day Dreaming', Suzuki Yasuyuki,
mineral pigments and sumi ink on paper, c. 1938–1940

'No protected world'
Tomas Tranströmer, 'Vermeer'

Behind the bare wall,
a laugh, a howl, a temple's bell –
then something began to gnaw:
the rat, beloved of netsuke carvers.

In a desk chair dying to swivel,
shipped from a country she'd seen in a magazine,
where women in the latest fashions
posed like statues afraid to wrinkle,

a woman sat defiantly still.
She waited, her hair bobbed and crimped
in waves Hiroshige would recognize.
Where were the foreigners come for the fabled silk?

She wore it spun into hose – though at the door,
she still removed her shoes.
In her lap lay a sketchbook, agape:
an open boat aground on her gray skirt.

A woman is an island. Beyond the wall,
her archipelago loved a border war.
The emperor wanted Manchuria.
What did she desire?

Wearing a blouse dyed a yellow
not monkish or imperial, she gazed
into some blankness all her own.
A scratching at the houseposts –

that stowaway brought by tall Dutch ships
to a port named Nagasaki:
the brown rat curled on itself,
a thing of beauty in the hand

of Death the great netsuke carver.
There, it waited for history
to require its services again.

DEBORA GREGER

Poem for Karou Abe

Just as against the bone-sundering waters
of the Shindo falls, or the Nachi or Fukuroda,
the itinerant flautists of the Shogunate
would pit their plaintive shrieks, even so
on weekday mornings Tokyo's enormous roar
is offered up the semaphored entreaties
of saxophone, trumpet and electric guitar
by the Mummy's boys that line the Sumida.
As we crossed the stinking river I asked 'Master,
how is it they get down there', and he replied
by standing his flight-case on its side
and unpicking the clasps. It opened like a door
into Stuka screams and Superfortress thunder,
a thousand banshees in formation over Chiba.

CONOR CARVILLE

Gilgamesh in Uruk

Forty klicks into enemy lines
a Humvee on recon
tilts into this city seeing
'dust and hajis mostly'.

Further back, a figure
looks beyond the wall
as bodies float downriver
nameless, unnumbered.

He had fought fire
and lost a friend
gigantic as myth.
And death was much
like birth, with its screams
and blood and tears.

TIM DOOLEY

Helmet

αὐτίκ ἀπὸ κρατὸς κόρυθ᾽ εἵλετο φαίδιμος Ἕκτωρ
Homer, *Iliad* VI, 472

for my grandson aged one

Its eyes are empty but the brows are wingspans
eagling over the low skies of the helmet's gaze

where tomorrow's battlefield sprawls. No wonder
the child is terrified. The bronze rings out,

a thick male voice sounding through the mask,
Wotan, Jehovah, Ogun. This is not the father

you love, the one with gifting hands and the look
of blue daylight all round him. But if the cap fits

you will learn this new language, how grave and gold
it tastes, inlaid with garnets and sagas, sunburnt,

sumptuous with works and days, you will see
with its eyes how gallantly the world is made.

LESLEY SAUNDERS

A transliteration of the Greek epigraph reads as *autik' apo kratos
koruth' heileto phaidimos Hektor*: 'and forthwith glorious Hector
took the helm from his head'.

The Shield

'I have no armour left, you have stripped it from me'
James Bond in *Casino Royale*

for Michael Hulse

Where are the footholds in this bright surface,
the sea-roads or star-maps,
and what do we women know of war,
its prosthetic arts and glacial edges

or whose mailed hands have stripped
the heart-leaved bougainvillea from our porch?

A mother plants her body – all its ploughed fields,
its blood price and bridal procession, its city
of labyrinths, its straight-horned heifers
and white barley loaves, its bluish vine-fruits

and the flute-voiced boy – between her son
and his fate. What we noticed was the absence

of yellow roses, the lack of gift-embroideries
or kiss-words on the threshold of his awaking:
the inner side of the shield is a pane
where he can see the polished blank of his face,

its stubborn bronze and tin and incorruptible gold.
He thinks of the flies in his friend's dead flesh,

the oiled and tasselled hair gazed at from behind
when he was living and strong. Then Achilles
walked along the shore of the sea, crying a terrible cry
for the slain, the sons and fathers of them.

The gleam of urns and lace-edged table-napkins
were our first books of light, the hurt shining words.

LESLEY SAUNDERS

Anniversary

My wife's father and my own uncle were in it.
It's still that close, that far away.
Millions of lives ago and a tick of geological time.
It's come around again, that day for poppies and
Remembrance. A hundred years this time.
What's a hundred years? What's a hundred
Thousand years? I turn a stone up with my toe
In a Suffolk field where my wife still saw
The horses plowing in her youth, not just in
The poems of Edward Thomas. The stone had
Been waiting for millennia. A man who
Knew three veterans from old Akenfield told me
Of his conversations. In the early days they'd
Take a village full of men together in one company,
Put them in a single trench. One shell left a parish
Destitute. Three alone were only left to tell him.
We wept, one said to him, not because we were
Afraid – we were beyond all fear – but because
We were so dirty, made of the same clay as
The long graves we fought from, lice in our hair
In our eyes, lice all crawling on our balls, and
Cold, cold – like stones in a farmer's frozen field.

JOHN MATTHIAS

On Certain Poets who would Write Poems against War

Some poets tell us war is shit,
then crawl like flies all over it.

Which war is just or just for oil?
I'll take my chance with ministers
to make the call, not those who spoil
good arts with arrogance and worse.

Edward Thomas knew that war is shit,
but signed up and got on with it.

JUSTIN QUINN

Domestic Interior

Let us turn, then, to the man and woman reading,
happy beside the waterfall beside the lamp.

BILL MANHIRE

The Hare

Leaving the house behind, and the trees,
we'd walked down to the bottom land
of salt meadows, marshes, dunes,
where beck looped out towards the sea
and sea-smell met ammonia
from the vast chemical works on the estuary.
A Saturday shoot. A line of men, guns cocked, stationary.
Wives, children (I was one), in a line of beaters,
moving over rough ground at an angle to them.
October, a sickle moon in the blue, barely visible.

A crackle of guns. The beaters re-form,
again over rough ground. Again, gunfire.
And then, a scream like an arrow through the head.
Two minutes. Another scream, and a single shot.
We broke. Somebody cried. A man walked back.
'A hare,' he said. 'She'll scream like that.'

In a couple of years, the barrage balloons,
ack-ack units and the boom of guns,
seachlights, bombs, ruins, policeman with a sack
of human parts, nights in the cellar, all four of us.

The pity of it, the pity! What had we been thinking of?

MAIRI MACINNES

Ataraxia

About six in the morning, light lemonish in the sky,
frost hemming pantiles and roof-trees
corralling leafy lawn, leafless sycamore, crab apple,
benches, the table for breakfast in July.
The big bare sycamore's hung with a dozen pigeons,
feathers puffed in the frost, plus – from an old gale –
two plastic bags. Now the sky's a blue in which
two seagull squadrons wheel in from the North Sea
fifty miles off, one overhead, the other diagonal.

Now new clear light fills garden between its walls.
A man emerges on a balcony, yawns, retires.
The gulls will be floating on the river now
among mallards and greylags, even a swan or two
(always food for a bird on the river).
But six or eight blackbirds sit in the crab-apple,
eating red apples each the size of a cherry.
And now there's a magpie among them,
flash madam, black, white, burly,
screeching. The blackbirds scatter.
The old woman in Number Ten looks on.
She's at the end of her tether.

MAIRI MACINNES

Flat Feet

My father joined the lines of enlisting men and was rejected
for his flat feet. A hand descended on his shoulder and a voice
said 'Good man' but he dragged his feet, probably despising
them, all the way home. My mother wanted to leap at the
news but a glance at his face told her she must commiserate.
Only when he was out of the house could she do a little dance.
All through the war, when he was in the Home Guard, she
kept up this pose. *He might not have come home, he might not
have come home.* Two children were born and they consoled
him. One of his brothers was killed.

I too was discovered to have flat feet. Immediately it was decided
I must learn ballet or highland dancing. My father thought the
sword dance might be best. But ballet won the day. *Tendu* and
rond de jambe solicited a little arch: air passed under the cowardly
sole that wanted to rest flat on the floor. Soon we were driving to
dancing competitions in the family's black boxy Pontiac. To win
the 'classical ballet' section was to release a dark shape lying over
my heart like a barrage balloon.

Did my father miss the colours and shapes of war? The khaki
and blue and grey, all those sleek seductive lines. The recognition
that we are dark within – not always, not every day – but there
exists a desire to tear down, to annihilate. No two year old should
be given a gun, psychologists say, because the mildest rebuke could
lead to the wholesale slaughter of a family. My father had an idea
of camaraderie deeper than peace could offer. My mother began
setting flowers on the table again but she did it gradually. She
cooked beautiful meals, despite rationing. The arts of peace
require such delicacy.

But there was something enlightening about ballet's relationship
to music: the beats of the music are not necessarily timed to the
movement that is being performed; the movement has a tempo
of its own. The music was a military band, jaunty and patriotic
and the ballet was women waving handkerchiefs that would
have to be put back in pockets. The spotlight puzzled me too: it

surrounded my shadow on the floor like the mouth of a cannon; there was no way to move out of range since it could track me down. Even though my big toe was pointing like an officer's swizzle stick and my slothful arch was as hard as iron.

I tried to say something about this dislocation in a poem:

At the ballet

Fast the pulse of the music
clear as a little stream running over stones.

Above the murmurous water the ballerina raises
a leg or arm, holds a pose that oversees

all that rushes below. Grace and poise
the fast and slow: one blessing the other

or each extending each: the music goes
on dancing in delight, the pointed limb

describes the arc the water would know
if it were slow.

But which is which? Which is war and which is peace? Is there something besides the quick and the dead? I'm inclined to think peace is the limb under the control of hours at the barre, the arabesque that tips and then tips a little further as though hearing a far-off music. While war runs on underneath, signalling into which corner the ballerina will dart, or the sweeping strings of the orchestra summon the ghostly Wilis into a ring. Peace has the ability to hear two kinds of music and war only one.

For if we respond only to the quick we shall soon be dead. But if we can allow its enchantments: the summoning of the blood, the ardent desire to act – if we can incorporate these as ballet music does there can be something more. The extended leg with its arched foot stretching into no-man's land where the spotlight awaits, the slow and hard-won patience, can have it all. That's what my father's flat feet – they remained flat until his eighties – and my arches – if I stood *en pointe* now I should break my neck – taught me.

ELIZABETH SMITHER

After Arnhem

After the night flight the silent drop
into the dark; after the rumble and flash
the holler and bawl; after the scramble
and crawl, the scavenge and shiver the slow
lying-low; after the shufti the recce, the trudge
to the edge, arms up in the air for the wade,
through chest-high black water, its slap-and-grab
chill; after the cursing, the cussing and praying

a yank and a haul to the back of a truck,
the weight and the rough of a blanket thrown
in, thrown over shoulders, a tin mug, a judder.
After a six-minute hero a knuckle-down slog,
shoulder to wheel, nose to the grindstone, up
by the bootstraps, never a word of it; schtum.

SUSAN UTTING

My Father's Parachutes

A cockroach scurried away
while the mildew got to work.
My father's parachutes were hanging from the rafters
in the barn next to the lagoon.

Looped swags, cordage.
He was dropping into Arnhem
on a wing and a prayer.
Pom-poms of flak, bubbles of fire.

He was dropping into our lives
with his trophies of war;
bringing a new war, which he won.
In a year or so we were gone.

My brain was four years old,
now it's sixty-eight.
The musty gloom, the drifts of tangled silk.
Were they brown or olive-green?

They have long since vanished,
shredded in the furnaces of tiny life.
My father lies in his grave
cut out of coral stone in St Mark's churchyard.

An awkward fathering, at best.
Him firing his German pistol
at a bottle floating in the harbour.
Him floating in the bay

with me on top of him,
his rubbery taut skin,
his body-hair tickling like waterweed, as I clung on.
Perhaps then, born of my fear,

the words he would claim later: *not my son.*

SIMON FRAZER

31

Manston

aircraft of wood & canvas drop off the end of the earth
'in the bright field' correct here & present
a quick wipe of the mouth

mix the hot & cold from the tap

in the days before parachutes
dinner a good thirty quid these days

as sea light accelerates up short
& then a stray bottle top scoots under the fridge – damn
these are the first air raids in the world

but which Fall album is best
the endless tedious debate

whilst the yellow paint blisters to the melody
Peel Sessions/Hex Enduction Hour/that disk with 'Cab It Up'

take the meal then push away the plate

which causes me to recall the last thing
my grandfather said when we left him at the home
'I've lived my life – now go & live yours'

Sopwith Camels shut out the Gotha bombers
shine brilliant as Icarus & phosphorus

in terms of practicalities we stop for a cup of tea
block out the damp & cold

which takes me a long way out
maybe swim the Channel when I'm that far out – might as well

a bunch of notes – transcribe speech & what is going on now
gothic imperial crosses float on the estuary
present & undetected
the aura of the material

what the argument sails through
dodging showers storms flak
on the Iliad dial

to brace embrace & cover the brain box
its contents light shifting with the water

surface impact accelerates – the mouth to its endless 'o'

a rough wine tinkles round the enamel cup
startled awake suddenly there are a lot of voices

'through eternity to the stars'

& the thoughts are beside me
like a nest of coffee tables – these are the conditions
drop away – a last sputter of German Romanticism

go a long way out – to the last drop

SIMON SMITH

USAF Ipswich

I woke and found myself indeed
among visitants from another world
larger than life, radiant, blonde,
rich, yes, close-cropped. Starfighters.
Yes, angels at eight o'clock, glistening,
and sparkling. USAF.

                Not flying
today, David Lee Woods Senior drove
a shining Studebaker, resting his arm
out of the wrong window and his hand
on the astonishing steering wheel
pommel, a mushroom. David Lee Woods
Junior and I, owning fewer years
than eight between us, sat in the back.
His exemplary mother. Family: USAF nuclear
Oh, capable! East touched the still
sea with light. 'Water!' he pointed,
a drawling infant in the flesh.

                    Even
at the base they had a fridge.
My father glazed in Ezekiel mode:
physicist, techno-fundamentalist,
an isolated Imam of a cargo cult
he was seeing the goods at last. Oh my,
America! These were the last days,
weren't they? Global and personal
terror, them, and us? O hydrogen bomb
come soon. Defend the people, scorch
and make pure.

          My family back there
to the London soot clung with white
unwholesome roots. Or, like spider-things,
great aunts in their webs, having
wrapped corrupt husbands and secrets,
waited for mushrooms.

DEREK BEAVEN

Summer 1962, More or Less

'I can cook better than you, I can love better than you, and I
can fight better than you.'
Barbara Stanwyck, *Banjo on My Knee*

Rough drafts of the harsh winds to come
ghost forth like the stuttering blink
of the zoetrope. The tall house in Westport,
    for instance,

that sultry summer early in the sixties,
when croquet balls mashed the sloping yard
to the reed banks, the walls a gallery
    of photographs.

Below the breakfast porch, town worthies
hobbled to the miniature post office
or up wooden steps to the general store.
    Was there more?

The private beach's maze of cabanas,
where through narrow slats I glimpsed the forbidden
of some cow-eyed high-school beauty
    blooming in the altogether,

or a Marine-haired local with a cock
like a fireplug. I had the night sweats
from the old *Life* magazine left on the coffee table
    in that clapboard rental:

the scorched earth of some Pacific atoll,
weeds brittle as coal, a few GI's
squatting, sharing a cigarette beside the foxhole's
    upright husk,

eyes boiled out, hands reaching
in plea or denial – what the flamethrower
left of the half-cremated corpse
    of the Japanese soldier.

WILLIAM LOGAN

Airgraphs

'nel mezzo di una verità'
Eugenio Montale, 'I limoni'

'Somewhere in Sicily', in 1943,
it went a long way
did army pay.

Under canvas in an almond grove,
there, you could solve
'your worst problem – washing',
as you wrote home to your mother.
'A local housewife is doing it for me,'
and her husband only charged 3 shilling.

You could get a new spring in your watch for 5,
which did seem 'very cheap'.
There were 'peaches, pears, lemons and grapes'
in Sicily, somewhere, that September '43.
Eggs were 'obtainable at 4d'
or 6 if you were foolish ...
and reading your airgraphs, dad, what I see
is a steel helmet 'always full' of lemons.

PETER ROBINSON

My Italy

'Pace, pace, pace. –'
Petrarch, *Canzoniere* 128

When the balconies blossomed with identical banners
all the colours of a rainbow coalition
in suburbs we wandered around street corners
where house-fronts were forming an apt quotation.

And though the peace party would inevitably lose,
I wasn't inclined to fix tired eyes
on anything else than flags like those –
that one word printed on them more than headline-size.

So we followed the parallels of apartment balconies
bedecked with allusions to a poet's words
in earliest springtime while flowering magnolias,

cherry trees by sidings, and sound-bites of birds
were also just responses to our long-prolonged cries
from the states' and petty tyrants' perpetual wars.

Parma, 22 March 2003

PETER ROBINSON

Afterwards

All men grew Peace, but none so well as you,
a silver cup from the local show
as proof of your endeavours.
I have all your garden stuff, you know,
daisy grubber, hoe, the half-moon edging tool
that still looks happy as it works.

The antiquated kit: the brass pump for roses,
your billhook. Mid cut, your rotor mower
takes 40-winks under the cover of the plum,
next to your enamel mug –
the brews that got you through the worst of it.

And always your lads returned,
eyes wide, still in battledress, still baffled
by the permanence of death. Standing,
open-wounded, blood-blackened,
by the fence and looking to you for orders.

I saw them crowded in your eyes –
how the western desert scorches, desiccates
the flesh. And so I keep the shed door
open to watch you as you graft.
You, Dad, in your element, lost to
thingummies, seed catalogues, doings, string.

ALLISON MCVETY

The Smallholding

When he weeded or dug the beds
to sow Swiss chard or turnip seeds
or painted or fixed the whitewood fence,
fruit would fall with small hushed thuds.
Hearing each drop he could've said
its name – whether Gala or Cox –
how sweet or green it was, and when
his wife's foot lands into the house
after her morning trip into town
from heel against the stone he'll know
whether the heels of an army will follow.

ISABEL GALLEYMORE

Milia

I
An olive-wood fire and the local
pre-phylloxera survival red against
the cold wind outside, which is enough
of being, as if it were so grand.

Night folds its corners down
the terraced hillsides and
walks upright on the
wandering streams, but

No sound, of stream or wind, reaches here
or almost, and the fire darkens. Breathe words
across my ear, breathe a fear, second by
second, jar by jar, fear of war and world, be explicit.

Let a resistance grow here, far
from world but close to mind, how
close it lies, to hear its breath
against the inner ear,

A breath to banish fear.
Then the streams flow on
and the air follow,
down the valley towards the world.

II
Thought that distils
against my ear a tear
for the time and
a silent belief in peace. Our cargoes

Were sunk in the seas and now
lie calm under tumult. Our dead
recede behind the night clouds.
Remind me of what I once knew,

Breathe the truth back faintly across
my ear in this walled shelter and hear
the plants shake, the earth tumble.
There is only one peace, a lot further out.

PETER RILEY

Special Stickers

Everyone's an expert and it's not just fear,
the idea of young men, and here's an intercept,
class system renewed –

in blood, boss.

Count the dead
by socio-economic caste. Work the silent and the silent work themselves.
You're thinking *Just look after your mates.*

I will be peaceful with you.

The idea of young women and an encased self for life,
controlled explosion. Man up,
girl: there are so many choices. Put the kids' photos on the device /
    point the device at the kids.

These are live experiments, unsold weapons on discount with a threat,
uranium's not a chemical is it?
so a little respect for peacetime full force, that's solemn practice.

Where's your sad face for schools? Special stickers in the pack.

RICHARD PRICE

Memorial

I pass it, most days, twice a day,
a column planted in front of the East End,
carved with instruments of barbarous play:
helmets, grenades and such. Nothing can mend
a war, no words wish it away.

'We must always remember.' And we do,
in forms like this, the dates
etched on the plinth in order to renew
awareness of what a continent's forged hates
resulted in, what young men then went through.

And yet we must forget, too, as those men,
if they survived, seemed often to do, my father's dad
being typical, who'd retreat when
asked 'What was it like?' into 'only a lad.'
It must have lasted centuries; was over by '18.

And is, I keep on finding, never over,
as when, dusk a blue ground beyond gaunt stone,
I climb the grassed slope and try to uncover
by scanning the design just how what's done
and memory's work involve each other.

I move away, the cold biting my face,
but 'merciless iced east winds' belong to those
with combat rights, part-buyers of the peace
I've known through wasteful, lavish sacrifice
this object with its Cuthbert's Cross would praise.

MICHAEL O'NEILL

Playing the Game

My thighs were warm under a lathering
of wool I'd plained and purled. Half-heard
as I joined front to back, a radio actor read
It seemed that out of battle I escaped
and I was grateful for the boundaried green
my son would wear it on.
                  Cutting thread,
I thought of mothers who had cast on yarn
against the Flanders cold wishing it were
chain mail. The worst of Bruce's fight
would be to be clean-bowled.
                 I pinned a sleeve
and coaxed a loop into the bodkin's eye ...
With a thousand pains that vision's face was grained
As I drew wool through 'cable six to back'
I felt with every pull at the shoulder line
an inheritance of mourning in the turn.
I feared that as he ran up to the crease
he'd feel the weight of that *retreating world*
and what was spoiled.

GILL LEARNER

Note: The quotations in italics are from 'Strange Meeting'
by Wilfred Owen.

Non-Combatant

I know nothing of war,
little of peace:
hawks and vultures
on the one hand,
doves eating breadcrumbs
from the other.
Pity is a plastic art.

In the individual
heart the individual
bullet lodges and
explains itself
at great length.
It knows what it believes:
that wars are made of words,
that contradiction
is the enemy,
that human stories
finally find their place
in heartbroken books,
that the great contraptions
of war are manufactured
out of god's irony for
the pressing of flowers.
That in the heartless aftermath
of nil and none,
on cinctured cenotaphs,
civic pigeons
murmur to themselves.

TERRY CREE

The Wound

after the Anglo-Saxon

1

You stare a pit into the ground in dream.
Your palms are wan. Your eyes are stream.
You stare a trench into the ground in dream.

> *Carline thistle hassock*
> *stamens of iris yew-berry*
> *lupine marchalan*
> *fen-mint dill lily*
> *cock's-spur grass pennyroyal*
> *horehound dock elder*
> *earth-gall wormwood,*
> *strawberry leaf comfrey –*
> *mix these with well-water*

This charm can be sung over that wound.

2

Then sing this charm three times over:

> *I have wrapped my love*
> *with invisible bonds*
> *so its injury neither*
> *stirs nor seethes*
> *nor the entry-wound spill*
> *or exit-wound seal*
> *for we must bleed*
> *freely over the field*

O, sing this over, love:

> *I have wrapped my love*
> *to rays of the sun,*
> *and feel it less than*
> *earth feels the moon*

DAVID MORLEY

The body is still the measure of all things

and we are caught between bright mornings and heavy soil.
The vulnerable change us
we steal their goodness which stunts,
our vitriol clashes against poisoned need.
Our separate torched wisdom shrivels before the defenceless and exposed.
The unprotected are not weak and their strength lifts our hearts
We hang back ashamed by our inadequate limbs
and abandoned best

ELAINE RANDELL

Peacetime

I
It had to be every summer, late on,
when the fair took over the football ground
across the road from the house he grew up in,
when the football season had ended, of course,
and before the re-seeding of the pitch, battered
and mauled in the rain-soaked, windy months of use.
From the bedroom window, atop a mid-terrace
of seven red bricked houses, he could see
across the walls and turnstile to the Ferris wheel
and stalls and hear as plain as day
the slightly eerie strained music and watch people
traipse into the old football grounds to try their luck –
pot-shots, throwing discs, buying candy floss,
riding a miniature Dodgem car, spinning wheels of fortune –
chancing their arm. Mothers and fathers and kids;
young couples; groups of boys and girls,
wandering about the place in the gathering dusk
of a summer sometime in the fifties.
He doesn't know how long that stand had lasted.
Did it happen there every year before the war?
That part of Belfast had escaped the blitz of 1941
but nearby had not been so lucky.
Had the families and crew who worked that fair
been doing so for years, decades, generations?
Whatever happened to them is another mystery.
By the seventies when he had gone
the fair hadn't appeared for some time
but he can see it clearly – the groups of people
squeezing in through the door into the grounds
in a kind of Fellini-esque evening light.

II

The background night is lit-up with street lamps,
and the amber strobes of the descending city,
and the mechanical chains and pulleys
and noise of the fair with its repetitive music
and the shouts and cries of kids and people strolling,
trying their hand at winning garish prizes
that everyone knew didn't amount to much
but who cared anyway, it was all a bit of fun
that came around once every year
when you were least expecting it,
the trucks pulling in and even parking on pavements,
and the fair being put up like a child's toy set
or a farm with animals and tractors and pens,
the Ferris wheel spinning above and over everyone,
unless, that is, he's only imagining it all,
and there was only a horse or two, a donkey and cart
and plastic mementoes like BLESS THIS HOUSE
or TO THE MOTHER I LOVE
like the steering wheel of a ship and the sound of all
the different stalls and the people milling about,
shouting in an excited way for things, knowing each other,
and he could see them closing up
when the night was over and in the morning
before anyone came back there was a watchman
wandering on his own through the deserted fair,
checking on things, going about his business
in the surprising brightness of the day
and everything looked very matter of fact,
mechanical, ordinary, so much more different
from the night before that you'd imagined
was a bit dangerous but there he was, one of the men
walking through the fair in broad daylight
with a hammer or monkey-wrench in his hand,
the sky mostly cloudless and the sounds
of the everyday like a bus taking the corner
at Alexandra Park, a ship clearing the docks
a couple of miles off, the sound of a transistor radio
on someone's back garden or kitchen porch

and all the fair's gadgets and tents and entertainments
standing there in the old football ground
silent and still until other people appeared
and started to clean the place for evening time.

III

For it was always night when they opened,
but he could be wrong, all wrong;
maybe the fair only stayed for a week or two,
maybe it was in August before school started back
and there was no Ferris wheel,
just an imitation one to attract the punters,
but no one actually sat in it and spun around
looking over the north of the city to the Lough
and the rising hills. But there was a man,
in the morning light walking through the fair,
knowing what's what by the looks of him,
double checking, seeing about something
that may be broken the night before,
he was definitely there, spotted from the window
at the top of the house overlooking, more or less,
the football ground, the fair, in the summer, ages ago.

GERALD DAWE

Belfast

The skies were less muddy than brooding,
with that crazed gray that promises bad weather.

Though the banks appeared slightly down at heels,
the city was bustling with new money.

Even the sidewalks seemed to understand.
Victorian offices stared down on the scene:

the cars overdue, like library books;
Celts in low-hemmed dresses, dragging

plastic sacks; tattooed public-parks too well tended;
scrubbed doorknobs adorning municipal departments.

The stranger could almost ignore
all that happened here, and what it was for.

WILLIAM LOGAN

Aftermath

On each weekly visit
to Shrubland Road, the boy fitted
his foot into the dunted place
in the grey concrete of the pavement,
its cracking and fissures
lined by browning moss.
After rains, its concentrated pool
contained the stalwart row
of terraced houses, sturdy
tiled roofs blocking
intemperate skies. This was
the street of the elders, great
grandmother and hair-netted great
aunts in nylon housecoats, determined
to wrestle days into conformity.
But the pavement's dunting showed him
the spot where the doodlebug landed
in Forty Four and sat, detonator
clicking into the silence between
startled house-fronts, for two days
(and where he lowered his school shoe
twenty years later);
before its nested threat to all this
could be disarmed,
the space of its aftermath discovered.

STEVEN MATTHEWS

The Word For It

for Great Aunt Kath

We were at Nan's watching Morecombe & Wise
when I was small and there

with felt-pen fingers, ankle socks, *Tiny Tears*,
on the sofa next to you.

Isn't this nice? you said and I should've
asked, if I'd known the word for it,

if there ever was enough,
maybe only understood

the thinness of its stretch
from your diary afterwards

when you wrote how my soft,
wise grandparents wouldn't

walk the mile from theirs to yours
the blackout nights Winston kept

Great Uncle Dick cloistered in his War Rooms
and you slept under the dining table,

the coupon fabric of your skirt
bunched in your fists like grenades.

CLAIRE DYER

The 'Stradivarius' Tree

'Put your finger on one ring – that is the British Army
going over the top at Ypres.'
Lorenzo Pellegrini, *Tree Picker*

Only Mr Pellegrini calls me this, only he knows
that what happened that day is an ache in my grain,
that it gave me my key: the long twisted C

and high C of the whistle blowing them over,
the blast that made a liquid earth, the after-shock
that fled as a wave to the borders of lands,

to this forest and soaked my feet with knowing,
made of me a dark house. With those notes
of mass a felling setting the tone for a century

I drew my rings close like a great coat, grew
through it all – height was the only distance
I could put between soil and crown. Lorenzo

would say that fewer branches make for cleaner
sound, but I ask you, what room was there
for tributaries, for light? War plays out its motif

year on year. The decades dry my heart, my wood
fills with a slow sorrow for the numbers. A great
instrument, like a great spruce, Lorenzo would say,

keeps its grief closed, works on it, lets it thicken
to something worth the listening. And its voice,
its voice will drop you where you stand.

ALLISON MCVETY

Quartet for the End of Time

by Olivier Messiaen

It seemed that the horsemen
had broken through the seals.

Men scuffed between huts:
snow creaked under clogs
that gnawed their feet;
breath blurred heads,
settled on patched uniforms
wrenched from defeated troops.

When the aurora borealis flushed the Silesian sky,
one Frenchman's faith hardened.
Because there never was enough
black bread or cabbage boiled to rags,
his dreams rang bright as cathedral windows.
He pinned eternity to a stave,
shaped hope in sharps and semiquavers;
shared his vision.
Cracked lips called birdsong from a clarinet;
swollen hands flicked at piano keys
to conjure gongs and trumpets;
fingers barely thawed
stopped strings
as two bows spun prismatic arcs.

Four hundred men
barbed-wired together
fattened on rainbow music.

    GILL LEARNER

Go into the Question:
What Remains of Mark Rothstein

What can we find out about a person we never knew, when
we go into the question? Sometimes, it would appear, very little.
Sometimes, too, as in the text that follows, some of the few details
that emerged during research have turned out to be incompatible.
Details are important: they are all we have. It was a given of my
task to notice them. Facts, wrote Hayden White, are events under
description. Technically, my particular site of remembrance on
the home front was not a battlefield. The survivors could have
been forgiven for thinking it was.

THE ROCKET

My second cousin Mark Rothstein died in a V-2 rocket raid on
London, the cause of death described euphemistically as 'war
operations' (not even 'enemy action') on his and his parents' death
certificates. He was 11. The V-2 was the world's first ballistic missile,
brainchild of Wernher von Braun: unmanned and unguided,
these rockets were so fast you could not hear them overhead at the
moment immediately before explosion, making them even more
unpredictable and deadly than the V-1. The rocket that killed

Hughes Mansions, Vallance Road, March 27 1945, after V-2 attack

Birth and Death certificates of Mark Rothstein, 1933 and 1945

Mark and his parents, Harry and Sadie, was the penultimate V-2
in the war on the homeland. It struck the flats where they lived,
Hughes Mansions, Vallance Road, Stepney E1, at 7:21am on March
27, 1945. There were 134 victims, of whom 120 were Jewish. 49 people
were seriously injured. The ultimate V-2 landed on Orpington
High Street a few hours later, killing one person, Ivy Millichamp,
the last (British) civilian casualty of World War Two. What a stroke
of luck for the Nazis that the V-2, designed for random terror or,
in Hitler's word, 'vengeance', hit so many of their prime enemies.
In the words of the traitor Lord Haw-Haw: 'Hardest of all, the
Luftwaffe will smash Stepney. I know the East End! Those dirty
Jews and Cockneys will run like rabbits into their holes'.

HUGHES MANSIONS

Hughes Mansions, named after the social reformer Mary Hughes
(who lived across the road next door to her Dewdrop Inn (do drop
in) until she died in 1941) was built by Stepney Borough Council
in 1928. It consisted of three identical five-storey blocks, each with
thirty flats, although three of the units in the western block (on
Vallance Road itself) were and are shops. This block was damaged
by the V-2 and repaired in the original style and brick shortly after
the war. The tenement-style architecture is typical of London
County Council social housing of the interwar period, although
the flats were the latest thing in terms of fittings: for example, they
all had bathrooms. The V-2 completely destroyed the middle block
(where the Rothsteins lived at number 38, on one of the upper
floors) and eighty percent of the eastern block. The remaining
twenty per cent was pulled down. In the nineteen fifties, a new
section was added to block one and a large second block
was built.

Hughes Mansions, Vallance Road, 1929, when new

The list of deaths reveals what one would expect: that most were in blocks two and three, although interpreting the figures is complicated by the fact that names appear in two adjacent columns: numbered flats and overall place of death, namely Hughes Mansions. Some people were found outside their homes. The Rothsteins, according to a fiftieth anniversary article in the *Jewish Chronicle*, 'had run towards the stairs, dying before they could reach what no longer existed'. Sadie was discovered at 18:20, eleven hours almost to the minute after the rocket landed; her death was registered on March 30. Mark and Harry were discovered at 19:20, twelve hours almost to the minute; their deaths were registered on March 29.

MARK ROTHSTEIN

Mark's grandmother Sophie (née Flashtig) Rothstein was an older sister of my grandmother Fanny (née Flashtig) Rudolf. Thus Harry, Mark's father, and Henry, my father, were first cousins, and Mark and I second cousins. Sophie, judging by Harry's birth certificate (where she is Sivia), could not write, or at any rate could not write English, for her signature is a mark (Her first language would have been Yiddish, a dialect of German with Slavic elements and written in Hebrew script). Mark's younger cousin, my second cousin Denis Davis, has vague memories of him at 'occasional classic Jewish family teas on a Sunday. He had a full set of drums and he could play them'. Leila Hoffman, another cousin of his and second cousin of mine, remembers meeting Mark: only once, although she thinks they must have been present together on family occasions, such as weddings.

Mark was a member of Brady Boys Club, the best known of Jewish youth clubs at the time and, by his day, no longer based in Brady Street but in Durward Street, immediately round the corner from Hughes Mansions. He is listed on page twenty of the March 1945 issue of the Bradian as a new boy, 'having been elected a full member of the club after August 1944'. The new boy was dead within a few days of the Brady notice. One former member, his contemporary Simon Palmer, remembers him as being 'a right little *lobus*' (affectionate Yiddish/Polish word for rascal).

His school friend, neighbour from the western block (hence his survival) and fellow-Bradian, Bernard Marks, remembers him as an extrovert and slightly spoilt only child. They would play a game called Wally, involving throwing a ball at a high wall. Mark went to Buxton Street School until it was bombed and then transferred to Deal Street School, which became Robert Montefiore School in 1950. Another school friend, Leslie Lewis (then Mendelovsky), tells me Mark was curly haired, thick set (like his father, judging by photographic evidence) and wore a lumber jacket. Leslie also says that Mark's close friends were boys from the local Roman Catholic school, some of whom would shout antisemitic taunts. Surprisingly, Mark even took part in fights against Jewish boys from his own school. Leslie speculates that Mark was reacting against parental expectations or pressure. This view is compatible with the suggestion that the boy was spoilt but interestingly complicated by his membership of the Jewish youth club, Brady Boys.

MARK'S FAMILY

Mark, Sadie (née Isaacs) and Harry Rothstein, are buried in the Jewish cemetery in Marlow Road, East Ham, known as the East London Cemetery. Interment was on Sunday April 1 1945, the fourth day of Passover. Probably there was one ceremony for all the funerals and, some months later, for the tombstone settings. Their Hebrew names, as transcribed from the tombstones, are Mark: Mordechai son of Hirsch; Sadie: Sarah daughter of Mordechai; Harry: Hirsch son of Shlomo (i.e. Solomon). Mark's tomb is in section R: row 21 number 1346. Thus, as the anglicisation of the children of immigrants proceeded, an initial trace of origin remained. The graves, which have survived well, are in a group of graves of victims of the same V-2 attack. The victims came unstuck in place and time: the wrong place at the wrong time: Lord Haw Haw's Stepney.

Harry's tombstone says he was 41, but, according to the 1911 census, he was born in 1900; his death certificate, too, says he was 45 and his birth certificate gives his date of birth as March 17, 1900.

ROTHSTEIN

פ	פ"ב	פ"נ
כ' הירש בר שלמה ז"ל	ל' מרדכי בר	ה' מרדכי בר הירש ז"ל
נפמרה י"נ ניסן תש"ה ק'	נפמרה י"נ ניסן תש"ה ק'	נפמר י"נ ניסן תש"ה ק'
ת'נ'צ'ב'ה	ת'נ'צ'ב'ה	ת'נ'צ'ב'ה

IN LOVING MEMORY OF

HARRY	SADIE	MARK
AGED 41	AGED 46	AGED 12

ROTHSTEIN

KILLED BY ENEMY ACTION 27TH MARCH 1945.

DEEPLY MOURNED BY FATHER BROTHERS
SISTERS, BROTHERS-IN-LAW, SISTERS-IN-LAW. RELATIVES & FRIENDS.
PEACE TO THEIR DEAR SOULS.

*The graves of Mark Rothstein and his parents,
Marlow Road Cemetery, East Ham*

Sadie's tombstone says she was 46. Their marriage certificate
of June 24, 1927, says they were 28 when they got married, but
Harry was 27. Mark was only 11 – according to his birth certificate
he was born on May 30 1933 – but the tombstone says he was
12. On his marriage certificate, Harry is listed as a commercial
traveller. Later, we learn from his death certificate, he was a
cinema owner. In between, according to Mark's birth certificate,
he was a draper's collector. On Sadie's death certificate, he is not
an owner but a 'cinema manager' and, indeed, according to press
reports, he was the manager of the New Pavilion Picture Palace
in Poplar. A search on the Internet reveals that the cinema was
damaged in a V-2 rocket attack on March 24 and temporarily
closed – only three days before the attack that killed Harry.

The marriage certificate reveals that the couple's wedding took
place in the Great Synagogue, 262 Commercial Road. In 1933,
Mark's birth certificate tells us, they were living a few doors away
at 292 Commercial Road. According to the electoral register, they

*Marriage certificate of Harry and Sarah (known as Sadie)
Rothstein, 1926*

Mark's father Harry Rothstein (on right) and uncle Joe Rothstein

were still living there in October 1939. Neither building has
survived redevelopment. The Great Synagogue was a constituent
member of the Federation of Synagogues, and yet the Rothsteins
are buried in Marlow Road, which is a cemetery of the United
Synagogue. This almost certainly means that the couple, more
modern than their parents, joined the more anglicised United
Synagogue after they married, perhaps when their son was born.

THE PRESS

March 27, 1945, the day of the V-2 attack, was the thirtieth
birthday of my mother Esther (née Rosenberg) Rudolf. I was
aged about two and a half and she was three months pregnant
with my sister Ruth. I first assumed the attack would have been
reported the next day, perhaps even headlined, in the press, and
that my parents would have read about it in *The Times*, which
was their newspaper of choice along with the *News Chronicle*,
judging by their reading matter recalled from my childhood
a few years later. But I was forgetting about press censorship,
imposed for reasons of morale and security. There was no
mention of the attack until May 11, three days after VE Day,
when with unconscious irony from the point of view of the East
End, Hughes Mansions first appears in a Times article headlined
'Victory Holiday Scenes'. The surviving block and the bomb-site
to its rear were visited by the King and Queen and their two
daughters on that day.

The *News Chronicle* reported on April 4 that all the signs were
that the V-bombing was over, otherwise nothing. Nor, unless
I missed something on the microfilm at the British Library
newspaper reading room in Colindale, did the *Jewish Chronicle*
publish a report until May 4, several weeks after the bomb attack.
We learn that this was the 'second largest death-roll in the seven
months of Southern England's ordeal by V-2s'. On the same
day, which was probably not a coincidence, three articles were
published in the *East London Advertiser*, the local newspaper:
we learn that the first doodlebugs (in the popular phrase) or
flying bombs (as the V-1 was named by Government fiat in
April 1943) landed on Grove Road, Stepney on June 13, 1944.
Now, on March 27 1945, Stepney endured the final day of
the V-2 bombings.

HUGHES MANSIONS AND MY GRANDMOTHER

The wedding of my father's youngest brother Leon was celebrated on March 25, two days before the bombing raid. Denis Davis, who was nine years old, remembers drinking lemonade under a table at the reception with his younger brother Stanley, aged six. It is almost certain that Harry, Sadie and Mark were present. Leon's widow Freda, according to my cousin Angela, recalls that while on honeymoon in Torquay, Leon (after hearing an allusion to air raids on the BBC?) phoned my father and learned about the tragedy. It was Joe Rothstein, Mark's uncle, who had the job of identifying the bodies. His daughter Leila tells me he rushed to London from Worthing after being informed about the air raid. As we know, the bodies were not discovered and identified until many hours later.

My mother once told me that my grandmother, her mother-in-law Fanny, Mark's great aunt, wanted my father and her not to leave the East End for pastures north-west following their marriage (in 1938), but to stay close by the two sets of parents, who lived in Stepney and Bishopsgate respectively. *Bobba* 'Dolf (as I called my grandmother) thought Henry and Esther should start married life in Hughes Mansions, which in her opinion was the best and smartest place in the East End. Had she visited the flats? If so, it could not have been the Rothsteins' flat, since my parents married the year before the Rothsteins moved there. Perhaps it was hearsay. Whatever, the young couple, determined for their own reasons to leave the East End, moved to Greencroft Gardens in Swiss Cottage for about three years. From Swiss Cottage, and probably renting from Henry's uncle and first cousin once removed, Ike Flashtig, they moved to 46 Boyne Avenue in Hendon, where I was conceived. Henry and Esther ended up in 41 Middleway, Hampstead Garden Suburb a few months before my birth on September 6, 1942 at the Salvation Army Mothers Hospital in Hackney. My mother lived there for sixty years. Fortunately for me and for her and for my father, they had chosen not to live in Hughes Mansions.

How little is known of Mark. He is remembered, and that is already something. A thousand miles from London, another second cousin of mine, Jerzy Feliks Urman, died (by his own hand) in November 1943, also as a result of enemy action. He was almost exactly the same age as Mark. I have far more information about his life in hiding in western Ukraine than I do about Mark in London ...

ANTHONY RUDOLF

Photo of Vallance Road in 1945 used with permission of Tower Hamlets Local History Library and Archives, Bancroft Road.

Photo of Vallance Road in 1929 used with permission of Tower Hamlets Local History Library and Archives, Bancroft Road.

Many thanks to the Borough Archivist, Malcolm Barr-Hamilton and his colleagues for their help and advice.

Photo of the graves of Mark Rothstein and his parents used with permission of Geoffrey Gillon and the Essex Commemoration Project.

Photo of Harry and Joe Rothstein used with permission of Joe's daughter, Leila Hoffman.

Retreat

'To muse on the perishing pleasures of man'
William Cowper

At the winter solstice, nineteen-thirteen about to end,
Arthur Wynne set his first word-cross for the readers
of the *New York World*. ('Leyton? Fulham? Hendon?
Ilford? Balham? Morden?') He lit a fuse. ('Poplar?

Is there really a part of London called Poplar?') The clues
included: 'To sink in the mud', 'A boy', 'A fist' and 'Such
and nothing more'. Today's—the quick one, not
the cryptic—presents us with an answer that fits, and something

peacefully opens. Aspens have already lost their leaves
as we advance towards November again. They litter the lawn
like yellowing news of combat, lists of the fallen, foxed,
archaic, reluctant to be raked up. They are the ones

that had been shivering even when there was no wind,
that have looked into a clear autumn sky for a con-trail
or a drone, and known that, as the laureate said, anything
can happen, in New York or here. I have already outlived

one that fell in the night with a crack across our neighbour's
garden and greenhouse, crushing our daughter's swing. Poplar
pushes its suckers through out of nineteen-seventeen.
It's daylight. A new kind of war comes flying over a school

as they play hopscotch, conkers, marbles, puff
the down off a dandelion clock, or kick and skip and make
daisy chains. Who's 'it'? What's the time, Mr Wolf?
In our time, poplar is unimportant, it has no heart

(except for pallets, pulp, or matchwood—it is slow to set
on fire, so upstairs floorboards, too—and it's used for veneer)
though once it made shields. Poplar yields before a blow.
Twenty-seven children maimed, and eighteen dead.

They lined the roads to Ypres, a tree with a curse on it, the tree
that refused to bow its head to Christ, whose cross, they say,
since nails may be driven into its timber without it splitting,
was made of poplar. Unloved, short-lived, for ever restless,

at its best in invisible support of the Mona Lisa smile,
or echoing a viol, a viola, Britten's *Lachrymae*. It listens
from its logpile as a madman whispers beside the Ouse, out
of his age's sudden enlightenment, counting dark lines.

JOHN GREENING

The Martyrs' Convention

The martyrs come from all over the country,
Some from abroad, the Middle East, Europe, Africa.
They appear the age they would be now
With shining scalps and gray goatees and ailments
They will nurse to covetous posterity,
Arthritis, bursitis, macular degeneration, the blues.

Or they look like they did the day before
Gun or bomb cut their last breath, clad in immortality,
Not ready for anything out of the ordinary,
They carry a pet peeve or rehearse a quarrel,
Not counting down their breaths, nor looking
Back as the only view left for them.

I do not expect to see so many convention children.
Here comes a group ropewalking in a rough line
Across the tightrope of this town's student-driver streets.
They wear their names on their particular sleeves,
Their hearts seem to panic like insects inside windows
But with excitement for an excursion from school.

All the martyrs walk a carpet made red by their names
Into a building whose bricks alphabetize the dead.
All the martyrs sport a ribbon across the body
Even if a limousine or school bus drove them here.
I cannot name them for I do not wish to claim them
From where they are now or for what I make them do:

Gather for a growing yearly martyrs' convention,
Robbed of a calendar and maybe even boredom
Whose high premium for them cannot find any cover
Except the sole offer of words of condolence
Wrapped in decorum like market fish in newspaper.
All I can do for them is read out some of their banners

Emblazoned with the places where they fell:
The martyrs' convention, Memphis, Keynote Speaker,
The martyrs' convention, New York, Plenary Session,

The martyrs' convention, Connecticut, playground symphony,
The martyrs' convention, Tallahassee, paper on self,
The martyrs' convention, Los Angeles, Union Observer,

The martyrs' convention, San Francisco, Attendee,
The martyrs' convention, Blacksburg, all disciplines,
The martyrs' convention, Dallas, Conference President,
The martyrs' convention, Money, Mississippi, Youth Leader,
The martyrs' convention, Iraq, another Keynote Speaker,
The martyrs' convention, Afghanistan, another Plenary Session,

The martyrs' convention, Syria, no safe play, no firm ground, no
   symphony,
The martyrs' convention, North Korea, Palestine, Liberia,
Testimonies of disparate, dissolute selves.
And here comes the tail end of the procession,
Ones whose ribbons are blank, for now,
The martyrs' convention –

FRED D'AGUIAR

Missing

Day and night I wait
for a word, not a
breath of air in the house, still less in what's
left of the heart, torn and dried out as if
on a rock in the sun, day and night tense
                          with the lack of news.
                          When the phone rings I

don't pick it up, for
fear of what its cold
voice might say, but when it makes not a sound
for days on end I yearn for it to come
back to life. I beg its harsh bell to wake
                          me from my mood. One
                          by one the days pass

and they all merge as
one. One by one each
dull task is done and my hands move on to
the next. Not an hour can be left free or
the mind will have its way. When sleep comes at
                          last it brings no peace,
                          for it tells cheap dreams

as if in need of
a crowd. The moon looks
down through a mist, held in the trees like a
ripe fruit in a string bag: one slice and all
might be well, thirst quenched. I don't pray, since it
                          was those who pray who
                          took him from me in

the first place. I don't
pray but I do dream
of how one day I might hear the squeak of
the hinge on the gate, and of how it might
turn out to be, not the boy with the worst
                          news, but him. When it
                          rains I hear his breath

in the leaves of the
lime tree. When it snows
the lack of a sound fills me with dread. In
spring when the slopes come to life with a splurge
of spurge, so that to walk there lifts the mind
                                out of months of gloom,
                                he is still gone. But

on days when the sun
comes out like a rose
and casts its rich shade at my feet, though he
is still gone there might yet be hope. He smiled
when I did. I filled his bath for him and
                                scrubbed his back. I walked
                                with him at dusk to

the view of the woods.
I laughed at his jokes
and buffed his shoes. I watched him dream in the
chair by the fire. Now when I lie in bed
with the lack of him I still feel his weight
                                at my side, a ghost
                                of him born out of

my own best self. Is
none of this worth a
kind word in the shops or a warm glance? As
far as we could we kept out of the light,
but when I walk to the woods on my own
                                at the end of a
                                long day, does no one

see me go by and
think, there goes the one
who loves? Would it be too much for one of
them, just one, to turn to me with old words
and say: Look on the bright side. No news is
                                good news. Take one day
                                at a time. Cheer up!

GREGORY WOODS

Leonard's War

'Greta, you can't, thankfully, see
I'm yellow as a daffodil! I wasn't, you know,
cut-out for tanks by nature, it's stifling in desert heat,
visibility practically zero,

the worst was dripping all over the gunner
(who's kindly steering my elbow now) –
those five offending articles there
look harmless when you're safely out

you'd've been sympathetic, dear –

these kind chaps are holding me up,
(though legs appear to be buckling under),
maybe you'd laugh at my lurid colour

something in my waistcoat pocket,
she's lit-up in Regents Street

stretching away, bowler hats,

Libertys' lights, her slant
on things, in deep
snow

she's wearing the cashmere coat I gave her

it's jumbled-up in a cold sweat

agrees I was not culpable
for this small mishap

foreign fiascos, but love got me out

this far ...'

KATE BEHRENS

Fire Fighting

Streaks of metallic yellow
in roiling smoke
are runners, tailfin, blades
of a military helicopter.
We're watching it
from a Bosnian roadsid
as *karst* scrub goes up,
crackling like small-arms fire.

This time, heat-wave or arson
is to blame. The air force
is strafing slopes with water.
Banking through incendiary clouds
pilots fix position, orient
themselves to shattered
farm buildings, abandoned
or dispossessed, ruins
of war or the economy.

It's twenty years since headlines
and euphemisms, sieges
and ethnic cleansing.
I've forgotten which side
of the IEBL we're on.
Embers blow south
into Croatia, Montenegro.

Shading our eyes,
half-deafened by the aerial thrum,
we can just make out the catch,
a dropped or garbled syllable,
in bystanders' voices –
those who'll remember this
as a controlled disaster,
as an aftermath
of something other, something more.

TOM PHILLIPS

As If Nothing Happened Here

'For years besieged from land and sea
everyone is hungry, everyone killed but no-one dies,
from the high lookout their eyes burn
the big flag and the deep-red fire,
and every dawn from their hands a thousand doves
fly out to the four doors of the horizon.'
Yannis Ritsos, 'Greekness'

Saidona is a mountain village of the Taygetos
in these places allegiance was to the KKE,
on the coast they sided with the royalists;
the pattern is an index of relative poverty,
as the hammer and sickle slogans fade.

Saidona was once known as little Moscow,
staring out in mid-air to an opalescent sea;
this is the buzzing spring of greening trees
variously excited wired birds swoop and call,
spreading flowers rise high into the mountain.

Saidona is quiet, far off a man hammers his roof,
the aconite, anemones and spilling daisies
dance at the base of the memorial's white wall,
an account, the many names, the lines by Ritsos;
and the sky opens endlessly to the whole world.

An old man came and spoke to us in Saidona,
he drew a battle plan in the car bonnet dust
– Churchill whisky good, German schnapps no good,
he made machine gun noises pointing downhill,
the date inscribed in marble is 27 March 1942.

Then men from Saidona died in the civil war
in numbers unmatched by any other village;
my friends have translated the Ritsos for me,
Lorna, Maria and Yannis living outside war
in the air as a medium offering no resistance.

In Saidona the stones speak where fathers hide,
at first after the wars, then from their children;
Eleas Noeas survived the death camp in Essen,
returned home to be executed in the civil war
and the doors open as if nothing happened here.

Ritsos was exiled and imprisoned on Lemnos,
Makronisos, Ayios Efstratios, Yiaros, Leros, Samos;
he thought wrongly, wrote wrongly and survived,
his voice sings out from Saidona, sings out from stone,
sings out in the vertigo of Spring on a perfect day.

KELVIN CORCORAN

A Video of Habima at the Globe

How elegant the discipline of your shapes,
        the line of the dance, the twang
of those exotic instruments:
        such gaiety, such impudence,
invented through a perilous history
        from Bialystock to Stalin's Moscow.

Here you are in London for a Festival
        of Shakespeare transmuted, say,
into Urdu or Chinese. Can his plays live
        using the guttural
language of the Hebrew bible?
        Your leaving Russia led to Tel Aviv.

That move explains these flags, loud music,
        watchful police.
That's why we pass through airport security,
        and so many people pack into the lobby.
A strip of land, hard-won by refugees
        has found a new generation of enemies.

Adrenalin flows in the blood as the crowd
        are allowed in to find their own seats –
we have been warned there will be interruptions.
        The play is *The Merchant of Venice*,
and these performers open with a mime
        of three louts bullying an old man.

Shouts rise as Shylock pleads *Do we not bleed?*
        but quietly protesters are led outside.
No bombs are thrown. The wiry troupe proceed.
        and the audience maybe warms toward
their nerve, the irony they give the story –
        at the end some stand up to applaud.

The actors bow their thanks, except for one:
     Shylock, a defeated man, alone,
walks off-stage through the auditorium,
     a single battered suitcase in his hand.
A chilling image – Could such exile come
     again, to those who worked to build a homeland?

ELAINE FEINSTEIN

Save the Feather for your Hat

Waterloo, of course,
another battle, a concourse;
the crowd, heading here, heading home,
a young woman, of course, another battle,
easy to spot on the concourse
there in her mother's plumed hat.

Too many little egrets died
for her mother's plumed hat,
another battle, there on the concourse,
too many to tremble the felt
with each rise of her head,
a young woman, easy to spot, of course
home there in the crowd at Waterloo.

Of course, she hunts the concourse
without sense, her simple face rising
easily for another battle, framed here
by the white aigrettes of her mother's
plumed hat, a young woman there
head spotting the Waterloo crowd.

Easy, another battle, mad to me now,
of course, as mad as Waterloo, Alice, honey,
as churchbells and afternoon tea,
a woman, young, on the concourse,
spotted there in her mother's plumed hat
with a crowd of dead egrets,
here simple and senseless.

She singles me in the crowd,
the young woman on the concourse,
another battle headed here
in her mother's plumed hat though
one easy look at my trembling hands,
of course, would've told her: head home,
spot there another Waterloo man.

KATE NOAKES

Czech Conscript

1942

He woke to the scratch of brushwood and a shower
of skylark song falling as the bird spiralled higher.
The scarecrow's coat had kept him dry in the hollow,
concealed his German uniform. Surely the song
was a good omen for slipping into France tonight,
that the Maquis would help him to England.

1985

In his breaks from grinding rocks in Sedimentology,
burnishing their colours, revealing trilobites, fossil ferns,
he takes up his violin, plays Bach or Bartok. The notes
spill out into the corridor, disperse into slanting sun.
Meaning music, I ask what he most enjoys.
He answers *Peace. Simply to live at peace.*

JEAN WATKINS

Suppose the unpredictable wave was God

We have been hoist by our own petard
What has caught us out
after all that was just our own fear.
To feel safe the falcon faces the wind
On the whole our backs are turned.
Catkin powder
dense, cylindrical, often drooping this cluster of unisexual apetalous flowers
willows, birches, and oaks
they stain her dress
O brighter star with keen eye
the day so much wants to see itself in you.

ELAINE RANDELL

The Peace Scroll

None will ever read it whole
As rawboned desert prophets clash,
The peace preserved within this scroll.

Inside a burnt-out hideyhole
A goatherd stumbles on a cache:
None will ever read it whole,

Though slow militias on patrol
Taste the fountain's cooling splash,
The peace preserved within this scroll.

Unrolled, an Aramaic soul.
Curators tend each burn, each slash.
None will ever read it whole:

The figtree shade, the bridal bowl,
A lifted veil and loosened sash,
The peace preserved within this scroll.

How patiently we must cajole
Word by word from dung and ash –
None will ever read it whole –
The peace preserved within this scroll.

ADRIAN BLAMIRES

Peace Camp

Craster, Northumberland, July 21st 2012

for Deborah Warner and Fiona Shaw

Rooted in truce
between dawn and dusk –
that was the design.
Soundscapes in glowing tents
on the gradual ascent
to the staggering keep.
North Face puffa jackets
essential against that breeze
off the North Sea, up and off
those glistening stones
that out-played the Vikings.

An emplacement in turf:
enclosures bedded down
into one dimpled searchlight,
giant and warm and still
against empty skies – the wind
crackling against the nylon
like distant returns of fire.
Inside, tracer lines ... *where the bee
sucks ... she is all states, all princes ...*

The keep come close to midnight
something out of Polanski
or Essen in 'forty-five with good citizens
fishing for home in the rubble ...

We pick our way back, heaving ourselves
over stiles, tripping on flints, keeping
strictly to the path created by the line
of stewards in luminous yellow tabards.

In my head for weeks not *come*
live with me ... but some
little-knowing king pronouncing upon
the sweet air, the temple-haunting martlet

PETER CARPENTER

Northern Home Front

When others volunteered in 1914, she would not let him go,
clung to him as fiercely as the children held on to her –
and would continue to do through all their fatherless lives.
Single men were called up in January 1916, but still she kept him
    close,
praying it would end. In his heart, he knew her sisters were
    right –
that, as a pharmacist, he might be spared in the medical core,
but he could not fight her fear. When married men were called
    in May,
he appealed – on grounds of her ill-health – but the temporary
    exemption
came and went. By now, he was as fearful as she. The children
    were old enough
to grieve. When he finally left for the front line, it was a matter
    of days.

All my childhood, I was struck by the stillness of her front room.
The children had children of their own: he was a photograph
    beside the door.
In a world, changed and free, she restrained little bits of
    rehearsed life
inside a small box that flickered in a corner. No new soap opera,
however long it would last in the future, could compete with the
    huge,
glass-faced, monochrome war scenes, hanging from chains over
    two walls.
No drama set in a north-west street could rival the one she lived,
    into old age,
blamed by her widowed sisters for causing her own grief.

The black and white screen's familiar characters, her one
    distraction,
were dwarfed by open-mouthed horses plashing through mud,
    stumbling, rearing,
as their riders' blades bore down on floundering men: sword
    against gun.

What always drew her eye, was a figure who staggered back into
    one picture,
head down against that of the dying man locked in his arms. She
    used to will him
to hurry, urge his horse to set its hooves in the mud, roll over
    and rise.
When she switched off the TV, this battle continued, saw her
    through the door and up
to bed. Every morning, until she died, she drew the curtains, let
    light stream
across a blank screen, thought she heard him scream above the
    rattle of her cup.

ROBYN BOLAM

In 2190, Albion's Civil Conflicts Finally Divided along Norman-Saxon Lines

I know your ancestors without researching them.
You were thick. We were thin. Fast and inaccurate
users of your landscape. Our progress started birds.
We descended, killing in our slenderness. Thick and
thin. Through thick. The thin.
        So far as I was woman,
I despised you in my heart; soon was un-womaned.
Quasi-indistinguishable among willows,
with superior weaponry, we kept on killing,
cried
      what must be victory
                with curled tongues.
Soon, you stopped sounding wrong.
      Young man, I am older than you think;
why are you sitting next to me? The art of peace:
scribing and diabetes. You bring gold. Thick. Thin.
Like a zoo lion's, your large, unexercised farts;
I inevitably breathe, breathe nearly the same air.

Let's start a conversation. Ask me where I'm from.
Where is home, really home. Where my parents were born.
What to do if I sound more like you than you do.
Every word an exhalation, a driving-out.

VAHNI CAPILDEO

The Dead Die Utterly

There must be a world
where the dead die utterly.

Where, when the final breath exhausts,
the man or woman utterly departs.

Then it begins, with photographs perhaps.
Holiday snaps empty out of faces.

The First XI has only ten players.
In schools each year class photos thin.

In libraries books erase their contents,
forget their authors, become blank.

In the cinema the latest releases
sometimes have a hole in a crowd scene.

But the further back you go
the quieter the films become.

This actress is talking to air,
she kisses it, misses it when it leaves her.

Give it another year
and this film will join the others.

Those slow silent films of empty rooms
where nothing happens anymore.

A.F. HARROLD

Quick March

Geraniums stood in ranked red rows
inside Victoria's railed parks
where servants took their Sunday walks
without an aphid on the rose.

My grandfather in brisk young life,
hunched in dugouts, ironed Majors' clothes,
spotted 'dead Jerries', when dawn froze,
then edged his lawns sharp as a knife.

My father kicked down Hamburg's doors
when they pursued the last SS.
He grew, in ground raked fine as dust,
long beans, parsnips, small potatoes.

The white musk roses bend your border,
bees bumble, where dusk's crickets trilled.
They marched; from rigid files, fell killed,
so you may garden, in disorder.

ALISON BRACKENBURY

Another Horatian Ode

Peace, great Augustus, can be yours –
    it is only an edict away:
        say 'I will not be Caesar,

'will not honour the poet who sings
    "Sweet and proper it is
        to die for one's country,"

'nor the casuist asking why
    our brothers call us, unheard
        to save them from the tyrant.'

Honour the Moon at midnight
    when she rules in shadow
        unbroken by flame or sword,

the city untouched by fire,
    the streets not running with blood,
        the forum where music sounds.

Celebrate the grape that ripens on the vine,
    the fish in the net, the lovers
        yawning at daybreak,

and the dreaming poet
    who calls upon you, Augustus,
        to be greater than you were.

C.K. STEAD

Rosa 'Madame A. Meilland' (Peace)

for Peter Scupham

You could in the last of daylight cultivate a rose
and name it for your mother, a ship in the bay
might sail with it, on the dockside, gantry and willow
could bow their heads. But no known prayer or herb
can prevent the coming night's invasion or fire
from flowering now terror's a spreading weed.

You could by the railway watch your child, who knows
all there is to know about weeds and fire, the way
their bayonets and flaming spires can swallow
a field in one. This is the new wild tribe.
From the bank they feel the metal's heat, the power
at which a night-time can approach and pass, its speed.

JANE DRAYCOTT

Two Poems

FACE

Idomeneus takes perfect aim
And hits Erymas in the mouth
And the spear penetrates the brain
And splits the white bones, and the teeth
Blow out and from the eye-sockets
Blood squirts and open-mouthed he
Vomits blood from lips and nostrils
And death's black cloud encloses him.

Homer gets no nearer than this
To the anonymous Tommy,
His human face blasted away.
What can surviving hands reach up
To touch? Tongue-stump? Soul-meat?
Homer's ghost has nothing to say.

THE TIN NOSES SHOP

Give us golden masks, eyebrows and eyelids
Hammered out of gold, and Schliemann claiming
'I have gazed on the face of Agamemnon.'

MICHAEL LONGLEY

Notes on Contributors

FLEUR ADCOCK's last collection was *Glass Wings* (2013). Her next book, *The Land Ballot*, in which 'Supporting Our Boys' will appear, is set in a small settlement in the North Island of New Zealand in which her grandparents and teenage father, immigrants from Manchester, tried to become dairy farmers during World War I.

DEREK BEAVEN was born in 1947. He has always written poetry but sees himself principally as a novelist. *Newton's Niece* (1994) won a Commonwealth Prize and was shortlisted for the Writers' Guild 'Best Fiction Book', *Acts of Mutiny* (1998) was shortlisted for both Guardian and Encore Prizes, and *If the Invader Comes* (2001) was long-listed for the Booker. *His Coldest Winter* was published in 2005; *The Icon Painter* in 2013. Derek was for some years a member of Thin Raft Poetry Workshop, Reading. He is married and lives in Maidenhead.

KATE BEHRENS' first collection *The Beholder* appeared in 2012 from Two Rivers Press. She was a runner-up in *Mslexia's* 2010 competition and other poems have appeared in *Portfolio – Dartington Hall Artists 1926–1987, Blackbox Manifold, Reading Arts Anthology 2013* and *Sitegeist*. A poem was chosen as Oxford Brookes University's 'poem of the week' in 2013. She lives in Oxfordshire and has one daughter.

ADRIAN BLAMIRES teaches Creative Writing at the University of Reading, where he is also working on a PhD in Renaissance drama. He is the author of two collections of poetry, *The Effect of Coastal Processes* (2005) and *The Pang Valley* (2010), both from Two Rivers Press.

ROBYN BOLAM's three poetry collections, published by Bloodaxe, are *The Peepshow Girl* (1989), *Raiding the Borders* (1996), and *New Wings: Poems 1977–2007* (2007), which was a Poetry Book Society Recommendation. She is also the editor of *Eliza's Babes: Four Centuries of Women's Poetry in English, c. 1500–1900* (2005). A new poetry collection is in progress. www.robynbolam.com

ALISON BRACKENBURY's eighth collection is *Then* (Carcanet, 2013). New poems can be read at her website, www.alisonbrackenbury. co.uk.

VAHNI CAPILDEO is a Trinidadian writer of poetry and prose. Her most recent book, *Utter* (Leeds: Peepal Tree, 2013), was inspired by working at the Oxford English Dictionary. Other inspirations include connexions to Scotland, the North of England, and India; her studies in Old Norse; and her time as a volunteer with Oxfam Head Office and with the Oxford Sexual Abuse and Rape Crisis Centre. She reviews for the *Caribbean Review of Books* and the *Times Literary Supplement*, and is a contributing advisor to *Blackbox Manifold*. Her work has been widely anthologized, for example in the Forward Prize anthology (2009) and in Iain Sinclair's *London: City of Disappearances* (2006).

PETER CARPENTER co-directs Worple Press (www.worplepress. co.uk.); he has been a teacher of English from 1980, and has taught at Tonbridge School since 1992; he was a visiting fellow at the University of Warwick and also taught creative writing at the University of Reading. Poems, essays and reviews have appeared in many literary journals and magazines including the *TLS, Poetry Review, Poetry Ireland Review, P.N.Review,* the *Independent* and *The Independent on Sunday.* He has published six collections of poetry, the most recent being his 'New and Selected', *Just Like That* (Smith/Doorstop, 2012); his article on the roles of creative writing (*'Singing Schools and Beyond'*) appeared in the *Oxford Handbook of Contemporary British and Irish Verse* (OUP, 2013).

CONOR CARVILLE is Associate Professor in English Literature at the University of Reading. Dedalus Press published *Harm's Way*, his first collection of poems, in 2013.

KELVIN CORCORAN has published twelve books of poetry and been anthologised here and in America. *New and Selected Poems* is available from Shearsman Books along with two major collections, *Backward Turning Sea* (2008) and *Hotel Shadow* (2010).

For The Greek Spring, a selection of his poetry about Greece was published in 2013. A book of interviews with Lee Harwood, *Not the Full Story,* was published in 2008. *The Writing Occurs as Song: A Kelvin Corcoran Reader* edited by Andy Brown appeared in 2013 and in the same year he guest edited issue 97/98 of the *Shearsman* magazine.

TERRY CREE is a writer and artist who lives in Hampshire. He has run a sculpture park, designed a number of gardens, organized poetry readings by many of the most significant names in post-war British poetry and has taught English and creative writing to countless numbers of young people and adults. His first collection, *Fruit,* was published by TRP in 2014.

FRED D'AGUIAR's sixth poetry collection, titled, *Continental Shelf* (Carcanet, 2009) was a U.K. Poetry Book Society Choice and short-listed for the UK's T.S. Eliot Prize 2009. A new collection, *The Rose of Toulouse,* also from Carcanet, appeared in June 2013. His sixth novel, *Children of Paradise,* inspired by the events at Jonestown is published in 2014 by HarperCollins (US) and Granta (UK). Born in London in 1960 of Guyanese parents and brought up in Guyana, he has taught at Virginia Tech since 2003. See: www.freddaguiar.com.

GERALD DAWE's *Selected Poems* (Gallery Press) was published in 2012 and a new volume, *Another Country* (Gallery Press) is forth-coming. He edited *Earth Voices Whispering: Irish poetry of war 1914–1945* (Blackstaff Press 2008) and published several collections of essays, including *The Proper Word: Ireland, Poetry, Politics* (Fordham University Press 2007). He recently completed *Crisis and Conflict: Reading Irish Writing 1914–2004.* He is a professor of English and Fellow of Trinity College Dublin.

MAURA DOOLEY's most recent collection of poetry is *Life Under Water.* Anthologies of verse and essays she has edited include *The Honey Gatherers: Love Poems* and *How Novelists Work.* She has twice been short-listed for the TS Eliot Award. She teaches at Goldsmiths College, University of London and is a Fellow of the Royal Society of Literature.

TIM DOOLEY is reviews and features editor of *Poetry London*, a tutor for The Poetry School and an arts mentor for the Koestler Trust. He was a teacher for many years and has reviewed poetry for the *TLS* and written obituaries for the *Times*. His most recent poetry collections are *Keeping Time* (Salt, 2008), a Poetry Book Society Recommendation and *Imagined Rooms* (Salt, 2010).

JANE DRAYCOTT's collections include *Christina the Astonishing*, co-authored with Lesley Saunders, and *Tideway,* both with images by Peter Hay and published by Two Rivers Press. Nominated three times for the Forward Prize, her most recent collection *Over* (Carcanet) was shortlisted for the 2009 T S Eliot Prize. Her translation of the 14th-century dream vision *Pearl* was a Times Stephen Spender prize-winner and a PBS Recommended Translation (2011).

CLAIRE DYER's novels, *The Moment* and *The Perfect Affair* and her short story, *Falling for Gatsby*, are published in the UK by Quercus. Claire's first full poetry collection, *Eleven Rooms*, is published by Two Rivers Press. She has been Chairperson of Reading Writers from 2010 to 2013 and is studying for an MA in Poetry at Royal Holloway, University of London. Her website is: www.clairedyer.com

ELAINE FEINSTEIN has lived as a poet, novelist and biographer since 1980. She has received many awards, including a major grant from the Arts Council to write *The Russian Jerusalem*, an innovative mix of prose and poetry (Carcanet, 2008), a Cholmondeley Award for Poetry, an Honorary D.Litt from the University of Leicester, and a Rockefeller Foundation Fellowship at Bellagio. Her early novel *The Circle* was long-listed for the 'lost' Man Booker Prize in 2010. Her most recent book of poems is *Cities*. Her autobiography, *It Goes with the Territory: Memoirs of a Poet,* came out from Alma Books in October 2013.

ROY FISHER's *The Long and the Short of It: Poems 1955–2010* is published by Bloodaxe Books. It does not contain the poem reprinted in this anthology. A second and enlarged edition of *Interviews through Time* ed. Tony Fraser (Shearsman Books) appeared in 2013. *An Easily Bewildered Child: Occasional Prose 1963–2013* ed. Peter Robinson (Shearsman Books) is published in October 2014.

ISABEL GALLEYMORE is currently a PhD student at the University of Exeter where she is researching ecopoetics and nature writing pedagogies. Her poems have featured in publications such as *Poetry Review*, *Poetry London*, *The Rialto*, *Mslexia* and *Entanglements:*

New Ecopoetry. Isabel was a Hawthornden Fellow in 2012 and is currently putting together her first collection of poetry. She is co-editor of *The Clearing*: a magazine of experimental writing about place.

SIMON FRAZER lives near the Suffolk coast.

JOHN GREENING received a Cholmondeley Award in 2008 and has won the Bridport Prize and the TLS Centenary Prize. He has reviewed poetry for the TLS since the 1990s and for the past six years helped judge the Gregory Awards. With Greenwich Exchange he has published *Poetry Masterclass*, and books on Ted Hughes, Hardy, Yeats, the Elizabethans and WW1 poets. He is currently editing Edmund Blunden's *Undertones of War* for OUP. Following his *Hunts: Poems 1979–2009*, two collections have appeared: *Knot* (Worple Press) and *To the War Poets* (Carcanet/Oxford *Poets*). John Greening's website is www.johngreening.co.uk.

DEBORA GREGER has published nine books of poetry, most recently *By Herself* (The Penguin Group, 2012). Professor emerita of the University of Florida, she is Poet-in-Residence at the Harn Museum of Art, Gainesville, Florida. She lives in Florida and in Cambridge, England.

PHILIP GROSS's *The Water Table* won the T.S.Eliot Prize in 2009, *I Spy Pinhole Eye* Wales Book of The Year 2010, and *Off Road To Everywhere* the CLPE Award for Children's Poetry 2011. *Deep Field* (2011) deals with voice and language, seen through his father's aphasia – an exploration of the limits of the self continued in a new collection, *Later* (2013). He has published ten novels for young people, collaborated with artists, musicians and dancers, and since 2004 has been Professor of Creative Writing at the University of South Wales, where he leads the MPhil/PhD in Writing programme. Being a Quaker heightens, rather than simplifies, his concern with the complexities of peace and peace-making. Website: http://www. philipgross.co.uk

A.F. HARROLD is an English poet and performer writing for both adults and children. His various children's books are published by Bloomsbury and many of his poetry titles are published by Two Rivers Press. Website: www.afharrold.com

IAN HOUSE has taught in England, the United States and Eastern Europe. His collections have been published by Two Rivers: *Cutting the Quick* (2005) and *Nothing's Lost* (2014).

GILL LEARNER lives in Reading. Her poems have been widely published in journals and anthologies and won a number of awards including the Poetry Society's Hamish Canham Prize 2008 and the English Association's Fellows' Poetry Prize 2012. Her first collection, *The Agister's Experiment*, was published by Two Rivers Press in 2011. The *Poetry Book Society Bulletin* said of it: '... The poems here fizz and crackle while exploring the vast range of humanity – they are by turns funny, chilling and angry, but are all diverse in form and content. [They] leave a lasting impression on the reader in this excellent debut.' For more information visit her pages atwww.poetrypf.co.uk/gilllearnerpage.shtml.

ANGELA LEIGHTON has published many critical works on nineteenth and twentieth-century literature, including, most recently, *On Form: Poetry, Aestheticism, and the Legacy of a Word* (2007) and *Voyages over Voices: Critical Essays on Anne Stevenson* (ed) (2010). In addition, she has published short stories and poems in many magazines, as well as three volumes of poetry: *A Cold Spell* (2000), *Sea Level* (2007) and most recently *The Messages* (2012). She is currently completing a book on *The Poetics of Sound*, as well as working on a fourth volume of poetry.

WILLIAM LOGAN's most recent book of poems, *Madame X* (Penguin), was published in 2012. Last year he received the Aiken Taylor Award in Modern American Poetry. His new book of criticism, *Guilty Knowledge, Guilty Pleasure* (Columbia University Press), was published in 2014.

MICHAEL LONGLEY lives in Belfast. He has won the Hawthornden Prize and the T.S. Eliot Prize. In 2001 he received the Queen's Gold Medal for Poetry, and in 2003 the Wilfred Owen Award. His editionoftheSelectedPoemsofRobertGraves(Faber)appearedin2013. His latest collection, *The Stairwell*, will be published this year by Jonathan Cape.

MAIRI MACINNES was born in Norton-on-Tees, Co. Durham, England, and received her MA from the University of Oxford. She is the author of seven collections of poetry, two novels and a memoir, *Clearances*. She married the writer and scholar John McCormick and lived with him nearly 30 years in the U.S., where she was the recipient of a National Endowment of the Arts Fellowship and an Ingram-Merrill Fellowship. At present she lives in York, England. Her work has appeared in numerous literary publications, both American and British, including the *TLS*, the *Spectator*, *The New Yorker*, the *Nation*, and the *Hudson Review*.

BILL MANHIRE (b. 1946) has published many collections of poetry, including a recent *Selected Poems* with Carcanet and VUP. He founded the well-known creative writing programme at Victoria University of Wellington, where he is now Professor Emeritus. Recently he has been writing songs with the musician Norman Meehan.

STEVEN MATTHEWS was born and brought up in Colchester, Essex. He is now a Professor in English Literature at the University of Reading. His collection of poetry, *Skying*, appeared from Waterloo Press in 2012. His poetry has recently been published in magazines including *Stand*, *Poetry and Audience,* and *Oxford Magazine*. He has been a regular reviewer for *Poetry Review*, and Poetry Editor for *Dublin Quarterly Magazine*.

JOHN MATTHIAS has published some thirty books of poetry, translation, criticism, and scholarship. His *Collected Poems* have recently appeared from Shearsman in three volumes. He is Editor at Large of *Notre Dame Review*. A novel, *Different Kinds of Music*, will appear from Shearsman in the near future.

JAMIE MCKENDRICK has published six books of poetry – most recently, *Out There* (2012), which won the Hawthornden Prize. He edited *The Faber Book of Twentieth-Century Italian Poems* (2004), and among other translations of prose and poetry, the poems of Valerio Magrelli, *The Embrace*, which won the Oxford-Weidenfeld Prize and the John Florio Translation Prize.

ALLISON MCVETY's poems have appeared in *The Times, The Guardian, Poetry Review* and *Poetry London,* have been broadcast on BBC radio and anthologised in the *Forward Poems of the Decade 2002–2011* and *The Best British Poetry 2013*. *The Night Trotsky Came to Stay* (smith|doorstop, 2007), was shortlisted for a Forward Prize and a third, *Lighthouses* (smith|doorstop) is forthcoming in 2014. Allison won the 2011 National Poetry Competition.

DAVID MORLEY's collections include *The Gypsy and the Poet* (Carcanet, 2013), a PBS Recommendation, and *Biographies of Birds and Flowers: Selected Poems* (Carcanet, 2015). He published *Enchantment* (Carcanet 2011), a *Sunday Telegraph* Book of the Year chosen by Jonathan Bate. *The Invisible Kings* (Carcanet, 2007) was a PBS Recommendation and *TLS* Book of the Year chosen by Les Murray. He writes for *The Guardian* and *Poetry Review*. He was one of the judges of the 2012 T.S. Eliot Prize and the 2013 Foyle Young Poets of the Year. He is Professor at Writing at Warwick University and adjunct Professor at Monash University, Melbourne.

KATE NOAKES, Welsh Academician, divides her time between Caversham and Paris, where she co-founded the literary association Paris Lit Up (parislitup.com). Her fourth collection of poetry. *I-spy and shanty,* was published by corrupt press in 2014. She has degrees from Reading Univeristy and an MPhil in Creative Writing from the University of Glamorgan. More of her words can be found at www.boomslangpoetry.blogspot.com.

SEAN O'BRIEN is a poet, critic, broadcaster, anthologist and editor. He is Professor of Creative Writing at Newcastle University and a Fellow of the Royal Society of Literature. His poetry has won awards including the T S Eliot and Forward Prizes. His most recent publications are *November* (2011) and *Collected Poems* (2012). *Train Songs*, an anthology of the poetry of the railways, edited with Don Paterson, appeared in 2013.

MICHAEL O'NEILL is the author of three collections of poems, *The Stripped Bed* (Collins Harvill, 1990), *Wheel* (Arc, 2008), and *Gangs of Shadow* (Arc, 2014). Recent poems have appeared in *English* Keats-Shelley Review, *London Magazine*, *The Reader*, *TLS*, and the *Warwick Review*. He is a Professor of English at Durham University. His critical books include, as co-author (with Michael D. Hurley), *Poetic Form: An Introduction* (CUP, 2012), as editor, *The Cambridge History of English Poetry* (2010) and, as co-editor (with Anthony

Howe and with the assistance of Madeleine Callaghan), *The Oxford Handbook of Percy Bysshe Shelley* (2013).

TOM PHILLIPS is a poet, playwright and journalist living in Bristol. His poetry and other writing has been published in a wide range of magazines, anthologies, pamphlets and on the internet, and his first substantial poetry collection, *Recreation Ground,* was published by Two Rivers˙ Press in 2012. Recent plays include *100 Miles North of Timbuktu* (Theatre West), *Man Diving* (Ustinov, Bath) and *I Went To Albania* (Bristol Old Vic).

ADAM PIETTE is Professor of Modern Literature at the University of Sheffield, author of *Remembering and the Sound of Words* (OUP, 1996), *Imagination at War: British Fiction and Poetry, 1939–45* (Macmillan, 1995), *The Literary Cold War, 1945 to Vietnam* (EUP, 2009), co-editor with Mark Rawlinson of *The Edinburgh Companion to Twentieth-Century British and American War Literature* (EUP, 2012), and co-editor with Alex Houen of the poetry journal, *Blackbox Manifold*.

RICHARD PRICE's poetry collections include *Lucky Day, Greenfields,* and *Small World,* which won Poetry Book of the Year in the 2013 Scottish Book Awards. Writing as R. J. Price he is also a novelist, with his most recent book *The Island* following the day a father and a daughter steal a car on what may be the last day on earth.

JUSTIN QUINN's most recent collection is *Close Quarters* (Gallery, 2011). He lives in Prague.

ELAINE RANDELL has written thirteen books of poetry and contributed to many anthologies. She has been writing since 1960s and in the past, ran Amazing Grace poetry magazine, Secret Books and Black Suede Boot Press (with Barry MacSweeney). She works as a Child and Family Psychotherapist, and lives in Kent with her sheep, dogs and other livestock. A new book is expected from Shearsman before long.

PETER RILEY was born into an environment of working people in the Manchester area in 1940 and now lives in retirement in Hebden Bridge, having previously lived in Cambridge for many years.

He has been a teacher, bookseller, and a few other things and is the author of some fifteen books of poetry, and two of prose concerning travel and music. His most recent book is *The Glacial Stairway* (Carcanet 2011). He contributes reviews of new poetry to the website *The Fortnightly Review* regularly.

PETER ROBINSON is the author of many books of poetry, translations, aphorisms, short fiction and literary criticism, and has been the recipient of the Cheltenham Prize, the John Florio Prize and two Poetry Book Society Recommendations. His 2013 publications include *Foreigners, Drunks and Babies: Eleven Stories* (Two Rivers Press), a chapbook of poems, *Like the Living End* (Worple Press) and *The Oxford Handbook of Contemporary British and Irish Poetry*, which he edited.

ANTHONY RUDOLF, born in London in 1942, is the author of two memoirs: *Silent Conversations: a Reader's Life* (2013) and *The Arithmetic of Memory* (1999). As a literary essayist, Rudolf has ranged widely: his subjects include Balzac, Byron, Borges, F.T. Prince, George Oppen and Primo Levi. *Zigzag* (five verse/prose sequences) was published in 2010. His collected poems will be published by Carcanet in 2015 or 2016. He has also written on visual artists, including R.B. Kitaj (National Gallery, 2001) and translated several books of poetry from French and Russian. His reviews, articles, poems, translations, obituaries and interviews with writers have appeared in numerous journals. An occasional broadcaster, Rudolf is Fellow of the Royal Society of Literature and the English Association. His contribution to the present book, accompanied by additional photographs, full notes and acknowledgements, is to appear – along with an essay on another cousin killed in the war – in a pamphlet from Shearsman books late in 2014 or early 2015.

CAROL RUMENS's latest collection of poetry is *De Chirico's Threads* (Seren, 2010). She has published translations of Russian poetry, short stories, a novel, *Plato Park* (Chatto, 1988) and a trio of poetry lectures, *Self into Song* (Bloodaxe, 2007). She teaches creative writing at the University of Bangor and contributes a regular blog to *The Guardian* Books Online, 'Poem of the Week'.

LESLEY SAUNDERS is the author of several books of poetry, most recently *Cloud Camera* (Two Rivers Press 2012) and has performed her work at literary festivals and on the radio. She has worked on collaborative projects with artists, sculptors, musicians, photographers and dancers. Lesley has held several residencies including, in 2013, at the Museum of the History of Science, Oxford. Otherwise, she works as an independent researcher in education and is a visiting professor at the Institute of Education, London. www.lesleysaunders.org.uk

SIMON SMITH has published five collections of poetry, the latest, *11781 West Sunset Boulevard* is available from Shearsman. He is Senior Lecturer in Creative Writing at the University of Kent.

ELIZABETH SMITHER is a New Zealand poet and novelist. Her latest publications are *The Journal Box: A Writer's Journey through Quotations* and a collection of poems, *The Blue Coat*, both published by Auckland University Press.

MATTHEW SPERLING writes poetry, fiction and criticism, and works as a Leverhulme Trust Early Career Fellow at the University of Reading. His critical study, *Visionary Philology: Geoffrey Hill and the Study of Words*, was published by Oxford University Press in 2014. He regularly writes about art for *Apollo* magazine.

C.K. STEAD is Professor Emeritus, University of Auckland. His most recent collection of poems is *The Yellow Buoy* (Ark) and most recent novel, *Risk* (the MacLehose Press).

SUSAN UTTING has taught poetry and creative writing for many years, chiefly at Reading and Oxford Universities. Her many awards include an Arts Council Laureateship, Poetry Business Pamphlet Prize, The Berkshire Poetry Prize and The Peterloo Prize. Poetry books include *Something Small is Missing* (1999) and *Striptease* (2001), both from Smith/Doorstop Books and two collections from Two Rivers Press: *Houses Without Walls* (2006) and *Fair's Fair* (2012).

JEAN WATKINS was born in West Yorkshire and has lived near Reading for many years. She has a degree in English from the University of Reading and reads regularly at Reading Poets' Café and venues further afield. Her poems have been widely published in poetry magazines and anthologies. She was short listed for the Poetry Business Competition in 2008/9, and her collection *Scrimshaw* was published by Two Rivers Press in June 2013.

GREGORY WOODS is the author of *We Have the Melon* (1992), *May I Say Nothing* (1998), *The District Commissioner's Dreams* (2002), *Quidnunc* (2007) and *An Ordinary Dog* (2011), all from Carcanet Press, and the chapbook *Very Soon I Shall Know* (2012), from Shoestring Press. His main critical books are published by Yale University Press. He recently retired as Professor of Gay and Lesbian Studies at Nottingham Trent University.

Two Rivers Press has been publishing in and about Reading since 1994. Founded by the artist Peter Hay (1951–2003), the press continues to delight readers, local and further afield, with its varied list of individually designed, thought-provoking books.